Closing the Book
on Homework

In the series

Teaching/Learning Social Justice

edited by Lee Anne Bell

Closing the Book on Homework

Enhancing Public Education and Freeing Family Time

John Buell

Temple University Press
Philadelphia

Temple University Press, Philadelphia 19122
Copyright © 2004 by John Buell
All rights reserved
Published 2004
Printed in the United States of America

⊖ The paper used in this publication meets the requirements of the
American National Standard for Information Sciences–Permanence
of Paper for Printed Library Materials, ANSI Z39.48-1984

Library of Congress Cataloging-in-Publication Data

Buell, John.
    Closing the book on homework : enhancing public education
and freeing family time / John Buell.
        p.   cm. – (Teaching/learning social justice)
    Includes bibliographical references (p.) and index.
    ISBN 1-59213-217-0 (cloth : alk. paper) – ISBN 1-59213-218-9
(pbk. : alk. paper)
        1. Homework–Social aspects–United States.   2. Education–
Parent participation–United States.   3. Home and school–United
States.   4. Educational change–United States.   I. Title.
II. Series.

LB1048.B84 2004
371.3'028'1–dc21   2003050794

2 4 6 8 9 7 5 3 1

Contents

Acknowledgments

I BEGAN MY CAREER as a journalist and college teacher nearly thirty years ago. For most of these years, the very notion of writing a book in any way skeptical of homework would have struck me as anathema. This book on homework would have been neither likely nor possible if it were not for a bit of an accident. In the course of a casual conversation four years ago, my former College of the Atlantic colleague Etta Kralovec mentioned to me that she had just completed a preliminary draft on the subject of homework. She wondered aloud if I would take a look at it and perhaps come to her class to discuss its connections with other issues of time and workplace management. The interest in the topic this manuscript elicited in me came as a surprise. It stimulated a collaboration that soon grew into a much larger project and an eventual book, *The End of Homework*, published by Beacon Press. Most recently, Etta has once again been extremely generous in sharing preliminary drafts of her new work on the extraordinary demands our communities now place on schools and the deleterious consequences of those demands.

Over many years, my graduate school mentor, William Connolly, now at Johns Hopkins, has forwarded to me early drafts of works in political economy and political theory. A first draft of an essay on the implications of recent research on neurophysiology for our understandings of mind and human agency helped me frame much of my approach to the topic of this book. Bill's playful and irreverent conversations about our profession, our culture, and our nation's political future continually stimulate my interests and give me incentive to pursue new projects off the beaten path.

I also owe a continuing debt to Tom DeLuca, now a professor of constitutional law at Fordham. Tom is a former graduate school colleague with whom I have collaborated on several projects over many years. Most recently, I have had lengthy conversations with him about the phenomenon of demonization in U.S. political life. Tom has called my attention to the ways demonization of the poor and ethnic minorities has not only pervaded our formal political discourse but also infected other aspects of ordinary life from schools to families.

Juliet Schor, whose work on leisure and consumption has justly gained wide recognition, has also provided invaluable assistance at key points. I first met her at a lecture she presented at College of the Atlantic in 1988. Her generosity with her own time–especially her willingness to linger several hours after the formal presentation to share ideas with my students–led us all to begin a longer process of exploring the connections between the work ethic, consumption patterns, and our schools. I have benefited from several subsequent conversations with her on related themes.

I am also especially indebted to Micah Kleit, Senior Acquisitions Editor at Temple University Press. Micah was instrumental in Etta's and my book with Beacon Press. His departure midway through our project for a new job was our loss and Temple's gain. He has encouraged me in the pursuit of threads I could not adequately follow in the initial work. His careful reading of the manuscript and many editorial and bibliographical suggestions have been invaluable. I suspect that few authors can be as fortunate in their senior editors as I have been. I am also grateful for the careful and prompt copy editing that Susan Deeks provided, as well as the production oversight and typesetting skill of Lynne Frost.

I would also like to thank Dr. Lee Anne Bell and an anonymous peer reviewer for Temple for many careful comments on the manuscript and numerous bibliographical suggestions. For someone who has spent much of his professional life working on political economy, the many references to works on the history of public education in the United States were especially useful.

Finally, in the case of this book, the debt to family is more than the usual matter of support and encouragement. These have surely been present, but there are intellectual obligations as well. My father-in-law, Anthony Covino, was a middle school principal for over thirty years and has long been concerned about the burden that homework imposes on all children and especially on those who lack appropriate forms of support at home. My mother-in-law, Mary Covino, was an elementary school teacher for a quarter of a century and often expressed her concerns about the impacts of home life on homework. Within my immediate family, homework has been a lively topic of discussion—especially in conjunction with the broader themes of consumerism and the work ethic. My wife, Susan Covino Buell, was interested in homework as a pedagogical and social issue long before I had ever addressed it in print. Each of our three children, Todd, Timothy, and Elisabeth, has a distinctive perspective on the issues discussed in this book. Each has often participated in lively intra-family arguments on the subject.

The concerns of all of my interlocutors are reflected in some way in these pages, but each will doubtless have reservations about the ways I have used their concerns and arguments. This is as it should be, for life moves in mysterious ways and always seems to leave some gaps. With luck, we can find more space for all to express their own doubts and concerns.

Closing the Book
on Homework

Introduction

Homework as an Issue
in American Politics

WHEN PISCATAWAY, NEW JERSEY, introduced a policy limiting the amount of homework in its public schools, the *New York Times* treated the event as a major news story.[1] A front-page article detailed the school's policy, the rationale for that policy, and the reactions of parents and children. Other major media quickly followed the *Times*'s lead. For the first time in a generation, homework–both its amount and type–had become a subject of national debate. I was fortunate enough to be part of the debate. A colleague and I had recently published a book advocating limitations on and alternatives to homework.[2] We were pleasantly surprised at the amount of attention our book received, but the opportunity to participate in this debate did more than flatter my ego. It gave me new insights into why homework reform is vital both for its own sake and for its connections to other related family and workplace issues. These insights have suggested some means and strategies for achieving homework and

1

school reform in ways that build on and assist related struggles to enhance the quality of family life.

Our first book on homework grew out of research we had undertaken in rural Maine. In a study of high-school dropouts, we learned, much to our surprise, that homework had played a major role in their decisions to leave school. Their stories prompted us not only to begin wider conversations with middle-class families about homework but also to explore both the history of and scholarly rationales for homework. In the course of our study, we learned that homework has not always played so prominent a role even in very successful public schools, that struggles over homework have been part of larger battles over how modern societies conceptualize and control time, and that there are constructive school reforms that might reduce the need for and burden of homework.

We suspected that our book would be controversial, but we were unprepared for the depth of the media reaction. For many in the media our whole message was translated into a campaign to ban homework. CNN invited us to appear in a debate, and prefaced the debate with an instant on-air poll: Should homework be banned? "Our" side received 38 percent of the viewer vote, but we were a bit taken aback that the whole message had been reduced to a campaign to ban homework without any discussion of the various alternatives our book had suggested. It became clear to us that there was a need for further work on this topic, work that would not only explore more fully the evidence against homework but also look at the reasons that homework had become such an emotionally intense political issue. Building on such a foundation, school reformers might address homework more effectively and build alliances around other reforms that are so necessary if schools and the broader quality of life are to be improved.

Our experience convinces us that the debate over homework is instructive for several reasons. Questioning the amount of homework currently assigned brings out strong reactions in many citizens, reactions more intense than debates about many pedagogical techniques. Disputes over how to teach math or reading have filtered down to the general public in recent years, but, aside from occasional grumbling about the new math or "whole language" approaches to reading, few parents seem prepared to mount the barricades over these. Homework, however, stirs juices. Virtually everyone in this society has a homework story. Parents have done homework and moaned over or gloried in it as children themselves. Most compare the amount and kind of homework their children are assigned with their own. Some parents react in shock and disgust at the thought of limiting the hours of homework their children currently do; for others, discussion about limiting homework or even eliminating it are long overdue.

Second, debates about homework seldom stop simply at the school door or the kitchen table. Many defenders of homework see the practice as intimately linked to key values of the society and argue at least implicitly that how we treat homework signals how seriously we take central moral values. Homework, after all, is work that a student does at home. Both work and the young have central places in our culture. Hard work was once seen as proof that one benefited from God's grace. Later it came to be seen as a way to that grace–or, at least, to worldly rewards. The young are seen as future bearers of our culture. Homework brings together central moral concerns about both work and the

young. It is thus not surprising that homework has become
a metaphor that extends well beyond schools. Preparation of
any sort for an athletic event, a public meeting, even a party
at one's home is often referred to as "doing my homework."

Even for homework's opponents, the topic goes far beyond
schooling. The language employed is that of the sanctity and
importance of personal freedom, family, religion, and leisure, the very goals some see as sustained primarily by work
itself. Homework as an issue thus becomes a proxy for large
debates about the future of our society.

Third, although homework in my estimation is hardly a
class-neutral tool, debate about the topic, as with many other
social issues, does not break down along neat class lines. As
I was reminded often, some poor minority communities in
inner cities beg teachers and school boards to assign more
homework. Their view is that homework is their children's
ticket out of the ghetto. Yet I have also interviewed and spoken with many other families in poor communities for whom
homework was the single largest factor driving them from
the public schools.

Middle-class professional families are similarly divided.
Some worry that homework detracts from the already limited time their children and they have to engage one another,
and they insist that it must be curbed. Others view homework as both necessary and salutary. Many of homework's
defenders like to point out that, while the time elementary-
school children spend on homework has increased, the time
those same children spend watching television has increased
even more. They go on to imply that homework is not only
the best antidote to television but also the key to our children's success in the global economy.

For others, homework almost becomes what one critic has called the pedagogical equivalent of the Lexus. Schools where homework assignments are rigorous and long are not merely a tool to master the global economy but a badge of educational and social excellence.

Nor were children a monolith on the subject of homework. I have had many adults, especially those hostile to homework reform, chortle and remark, "Boy, children must sure love your message." Such a rejoinder itself reflects a subtle cynicism about the goals and motivations of our children. Some children have ardently defended homework. One fifth-grader wrote to the *New York Times* in opposition to Piscataway's homework policy:

> I am a fifth grade student in Dutchess County, New York. Regarding your October 10 front-page article about the school board that limited homework. . . . I think that having regular homework until 10:45 p.m. and then having to practice an instrument is terrible. But I also think the school went a little too far when it prohibited teachers from grading homework. What is the point of homework if it isn't corrected? At my public school in Red Hook, the Homework policy is: third grade, 30 minutes, fourth grade, 40 minutes, fifth grade, 50 minutes; and so on. That is a better policy because it is just enough to reinforce the concepts learned in school, but not so much that it makes us have to choose between getting a good night's sleep and practicing our instruments, in my case the trumpet.[3]

But a Canadian youngster, writing to CBC radio about homework, commented:

> Homework is one thing the average student dislikes a lot. The average student spends about eighteen and a half days a year

doing homework. Instead of doing homework you could be doing other things that are just as educational but much more interesting. Building models helps you learn to use your hands and mind together. . . . Building toys such as Legos and K'nex helps you learn how to design and make your own creation. Drawing will help you when you have to make a sketch. . . . Tobogganing teaches you . . . about friction. . . .[4]

One network-news producer nicely captured many of the conflicts implicit in this middle-class dialogue in a conversation with me: "Why should I worry if high school children are doing sixty hours of academic work a week? I hardly know anyone in my business doing fewer than that. But perhaps if there is something wrong with what we are doing to ourselves, there's a problem with the demands we force upon our children."

I remain convinced that homework as currently constituted is a largely ineffective and overly burdensome practice. It not only creates especially serious barriers for poor families but also unnecessarily limits other forms of personal development and leisure time that are essential even to education and working life themselves. Homework is also a pivotal issue in the United States today because the families asked to monitor and assist in homework are increasingly burdened by the demands of their own jobs. Homework is closely connected to and rationalized by all the demands on family time, and the time has come to examine those demands.

Thus, building an effective case against homework involves more than posing dueling academic studies. Though these studies, many even by professed proponents of homework, have yielded confused and conflicting findings, homework cannot be refuted with some statistical smoking gun. Once we move beyond the controlled trials and the statistical evidence, developments in current learning theory and classroom practice can tell us about how children learn. On that basis we can explore just why homework is unlikely to work as advertised. But just as importantly, we can then build constructive alternatives to homework on this foundation. Chapter 1, "Revisiting the Evidence," strives to broaden the academic debate about the efficacy of homework by examining not only the many trials regarding homework's efficacy but also related work in learning theory and neurophysiology.

These first skirmishes in the homework wars also teach another lesson. Homework cannot be dissociated from our larger cultural dreams and anxieties about work itself. An exploration of the history of homework must place that history in the large context of the history of work itself. As Chapter 2 suggests, homework is part of a larger story about the cultural and political battles over the control of time itself.

That history clearly shows the connections of homework to the emergence of our modern global capitalism. Today's debates are framed by constant rhetoric about success in the global economy. Whatever homework's history or its failings and costs, it is likely to be retained as a practice as long as most of us are convinced that it is the only way to convey life long skills or character lessons essential to our survival. But if homework hardly assures success in the global economy, and if work without end is not the only way to live a constructive, civilized life, then homework reform should hardly be anathema. Indeed, educational reforms that both free family time and foster more adequate and equal education would not only improve our quality of life. They could also facilitate needed inquiry into the reasons for the loss of free time in many areas of American life. Chapter 3 places homework reform in the context of emerging debates about global capitalism, working hours, and the quality of family life. In the process, it helps shed new light on debates in each area.

Homework reform poses challenges both to current educational practice and to prevalent notions of personal development. Homework reform is unlikely to take root until educators can not only understand its limits but also have clearer notions of how schools and classrooms can be organized without extensive reliance on homework as we know it. As I suggest in Chapter 4, U.S. public schools are not the disaster they are often portrayed as. Nor can the problems from which they do suffer be alleviated by adding more homework.

Finally, no assessment of this issue is complete without assessing the issue of character. Schools that foster student development by means other than homework do not undermine the kind of character development necessary to sustain a functioning democracy. The debate on homework can be more fruitful for all partisans if all can stake out more fully the political, educational, and moral ideals implicated in the debate.

I take a position on this pivotal issue in the concluding chapter.

1

Revisiting the Evidence

FOR A PRACTICE as solidly entrenched as homework, the scholarly case on its behalf is surprisingly weak and even contradictory. Much of the popular media's support for homework is based on the assumption that the practice has been tested and found essential to academic success. Yet scholarly studies of homework's ability to deliver in even such short-term and narrow areas as test scores and grades yield at best uneven results. In addition, homework's advocates often fail to assess not only the long-term effects of the practice but also the implications modern learning theory has in the debate.

The controversy over homework starts with a large number of academic studies that have sought to establish or refute the notion that homework improves academic performance. My colleague and I pointed out in previous work on this topic that many studies purporting to establish the efficacy of homework demonstrate at best a correlation between hours of homework and academic performance. That is, they show that those students who do homework receive better grades or higher test scores, but they do not establish that homework causes improved performance.

Some defenders of homework have acknowledged this limitation to many earlier studies but have then gone on to suggest that we are "desperate" to find alternative explanations for why students in the studies who did more homework also received better grades. They argue that common sense tells us that homework is a major cause of academic success.

Yet the case against homework hardly stops with the problem of assuming that, merely because student A does more homework than student B and receives a better grade, homework was the cause. Homework defenders fail to acknowledge that many other studies of homework show no correlation—or even indicate an inverse relationship—between homework and students' performance.

Over the years, homework has been subjected to a series of controlled trials. These trials vary considerably in their attempts to control for such confounding variables as the education and wealth of the parents. Bringing together all such trials into the kind of meta-analysis often attempted with respect to drugs is a difficult task, but one respected investigator has done it. Harris Cooper reports: "The conclusions of past reviewers of homework research show extraordinary variability.... Even in regard to specific areas of application such as within different subject areas, grades or student ability levels, the reviews often directly contradict one another." Cooper, who is a strong advocate of homework, also points out that "increasing the amount of homework for middle school students may be efficacious up to a certain point, but after that point more time spent on assignments is of no value. There is no evidence that any amount of homework improves the academic performance of elementary school students."[1]

Even more telling, homework advocates now also concede that their research is culturally relative. Thus, Cooper's own meta-analysis of homework studies leaves out all studies conducted before 1962. He makes the point that "educational, familial, and social patterns of behavior have changed enough in the past quarter century that data from earlier studies is likely to have questionable relevance to decisions made about homework today."[2]

Here Cooper is acknowledging a fundamental dilemma of the social sciences. The research is conducted on subjects who are not uniform across time and space. They develop ideas and expectations of their own and can be influenced in a variety of ways even by research agendas themselves. Homework may indeed "work" on one set of students but fail to work on another because of the varying sets of expectations and experiences brought to that homework.

This comment is not meant to suggest that "wishing makes it so," but it does imply that all research about homework needs to be set in terms of the assumptions and ideals all actors bring to it. Thus, any politics of homework needs to consider the place of homework in the larger culture.

In this context, Cooper correctly assumes major cultural differences between 1962 and his 1989 study. Nevertheless, his point needs to be pushed further. Should one assume that in 2001 we can speak of a uniform U.S. culture? Perhaps one difference between today and 1962 is that our culture is both more diverse and subject to more rapid change. Perhaps the very idea of the need for one mandated statewide, or even district-wide, homework policy needs to be questioned, especially if some parents and children are both skeptical of its positive effects and bitter about the demands it places on limited family time while others regard homework as the anchor and symbol of morality itself.

It is also interesting that almost all of the tests of homework measure its success in terms of its ability either to improve grades in the current course or to increase scores on standardized tests taken shortly after a homework regime has been instituted. Such procedures simply assume that better grades or test scores are a good predictor of a student's ability to retain and use bodies of knowledge at later points in his or her life. Yet grades are at best one of many indicators of a student's ability to use and retain knowledge. In addition, for some of the homework studies, the researcher was also the teacher in the course under study. That the researcher's biases may have entered into how experimental and research groups were taught is a possibility that is inadequately considered in many of these studies. As for the use of standardized tests as a measure of success, even for such staples of standardized testing as the SATs, long-term predictability has not been achieved. Scores on these tests serve only as a marker for grades in the first year of college.[3]

Although I have qualms about using one standardized test as a measure of academic excellence, even if one accepts that gauge, one cannot conclude that homework is the primary agent producing educational excellence. In the broadest measure, the *Third International Math and Science Study* in 1995, there was no demonstrable link between homework and achievement. In fact, Japanese eighth-graders received less homework and outperformed their U.S. counterparts.[4]

Homework defenders' use of the common-sense argument itself merits closer attention. Does "time on task" always improve performance? I find it interesting that, just as the debate about homework has been heating up, the popular press has also run stories about increasing public and government interest in the phenomenon of medical errors. Careful studies of hospital records now indicate that the number of accidental and preventable deaths in hospitals is far greater than once imagined. Research on the causes of these deaths is at an early stage, but the "common sense" of many scholars is that fatigue on the part of medical personnel is a major cause of the problem. Important information from patients is not absorbed or is imperfectly understood by tired physicians, and nurses charged with the task of overseeing patient care are often at the end of very long working days. A study conducted by the *American Journal of Public Health* in 1992 found that nurses in Massachusetts who work variable schedules (including mandated overtime shifts) were twice as likely to report an accident or error and two-and-one-half times as likely to report near-miss accidents. It concluded that these conditions were associated with "frequent lapses of attention and increased reaction time, leading to increased error rates on performance of tasks."[5]

Some, of course, will argue that this example is irrelevant. Nurses are asked to work fifteen-hour shifts,and emergency-room residents notoriously work shifts as long as eighty hours per week. A third-grader may work thirty-one or thirty-two hours in school and then be asked, under current National Education Association guidelines, to do another two and a half hours of homework per week. What's the big deal?

Modern physicians are trained from medical school for the rigors of long hours, but many clearly reach a saturation point beyond which absorbing new information becomes virtually impossible. Young children reach a saturation point far more quickly than adults. Beyond the hours spent in school itself, the young child faces an average commuting time of about three hours a week, time spent in getting ready for school, and meal times. In today's households, even most young children have some household chores, as well. With these demands on young children, fatigue and an inability to sustain concentration is likely to be a substantial factor in learning. Such fatigue may well mean not merely that a law of diminishing returns is soon encountered. Misinformation may be absorbed, and confusion and frustration can affect long-term interest in the subject matter.

Systematic studies of homework's long-term effects are especially inadequate. Even Cooper points out that "only a few studies looked at homework's effect on attitudes toward school (with generally negligible results). No studies looked at non-academic outcomes like study habits, cheating, or participation in community activities."[6]

Direct evidence for these scores may be lacking. The long-standing discussion of the predictive role of another staple of U.S. education, the SAT, however, has yielded other questions. Anecdotally, many school administrators note that some of their greatest success stories come not from those who spent the many hours studying to get high SAT scores but from those who have enjoyed a wealth of life experience, including participation in community-service activities. The very absence of studies assessing homework's impact on love of life-long learning or on community involvement says something about how a prevailing cultural mindset has guided research and discussions of this topic.

Current discussions of homework also raise the issue of its class biases. Defenders of homework argue that parents in many poor communities want their children to be assigned substantial homework so they can develop self-esteem and the skills needed to escape their economic plight. I will assess the historical reasons for these requests and my concerns about them more fully in subsequent chapters, but once again all claims that homework critiques involve a war against the poor systematically disregard important evidence.

Our own work began with an ethnographic study of high-school dropouts in rural Maine. In the course of our work we asked each of the students whether they could identify a point in their educational careers at which they knew they were not going to make it through school. To our surprise, every student included as one primary reason for dropping out the inability to complete homework assignments. Nor were their stories of the dog-ate-my-homework sort. Students identified a range of factors, including absence of secure and quiet spaces in which to do the work, economic responsibilities for other siblings, lack of parental help, and lack of academic resources. In many instances, the adults who worked with these teenagers on a regular basis confirmed the reports that they provided.

That homework may be something less than a panacea for the poor is suggested in other ways, as well. One of the most startling features of the current scene is the suggestion by some urban school principals that teachers assign "parent-neutral" homework. Parent-neutral homework is the kind of work that teachers can assign with assurance that any child can do equally well, regardless of the formal knowledge or involvement of the parent.

At this point I am not aware of a literature delineating parent-neutral homework and showing its clear efficacy. One would wonder, for instance, whether diluting homework so much that any child can do it without assistance from an adult results in exercises that really benefit the child. Articulated concerns about parent-neutral homework, along with the proliferation of after-school programs aimed at helping children with homework, do suggest that current homework practices are failing to achieve their stated ends.

Recognizing gaps in the homework research, the more thoughtful homework advocates have two fall-back positions. They simply assert its positive effects on character or they redefine homework. Thus, Cooper fully concedes that "teachers should not assign homework to young children with the expectation that it will noticeably enhance achievement. Instead, teachers might assign short and simple homework to younger students, *hoping* it will foster positive, long term educational behaviors and attitudes."[7] Yet as we have noticed, Cooper himself concedes that the research on homework's effects on long-term attitudes is not there. He is expressing a hope without even asking whether means other than homework might better instill time-management and character skills than giving students assignments that admittedly do not improve their performance.

Homework advocates such as Cooper also argue that research demonstrates that homework's positive effects are enhanced when parents are at least available to encourage or monitor its completion. They also argue that, for older children, homework may appropriately involve more complex assignments. Yet many homework advocates also now acknowledge that for some parents, even those with the best intentions, it is hard to be available to monitor homework and even more difficult to provide assistance on complex tasks. They then fall back on a major reconceptualization of homework. Yes, some say, current homework creates problems for some children, but the best approach is to individualize homework. Thus, Cooper now suggests that teachers consider each child's personal and family situation and calibrate the kinds and amount of homework accordingly.[8] Even if teachers in most large classrooms were in a position to pursue this strategy, it raises important concerns about the further class stratification of American education. What if those children who already benefit from formally educated parents and ample facilities are then given the complex assignments while others are given only very simple ones? What does this practice do to the educational development and self-esteem of those assigned simple rote work? If independent and self-directed work is best calibrated to the individual student, why does it not make more sense to have teachers or other well-trained adults more actively involved with all individual students?

Even in pedagogical terms, the debate over homework has been cast in too narrow terms. Beyond dueling trials on the efficacy of homework, learning theory now has implications for this debate. Let me start with a homely example of very basic learning theory recently cited by a leading educator, Susan Ohanian.

For most of the past generation, pediatricians and other child-care "experts" have suggested that most infants have an appropriate age for weaning and another appropriate age for toilet training. Ohanian points to work in current pediatric literature, and to that of the child-care expert T. Berry Brazelton, rejecting such invariant notions of learning development. "Brazelton observes that some children are ready to use the potty at age two; others are ready at age four," Ohanian says. "And guess what? Those who wait until four soon become just as adept in the bathroom as those precocious early pottyers. Brazelton says that children who are allowed to learn potty use at their own pace gain a sense of accomplishment that's lost when pushy parents resort to threats and bribes."[9]

This insight about early-childhood development has important analogues for learning theory in the later years. Building on the foundation laid by Jean Piaget, educators now recognize that cognitive structures develop and change over the course of an individual child's maturation. The level of this development determines the child's problem-solving abilities. Thus, in the name of learning new things, educators must scaffold new learning onto existing mental frameworks.

Piaget suggests that requiring every child in a given grade to perform uniform tasks—demanded by many homework assignments—before some are developmentally ready is counterproductive. For a teacher, understanding a student's level of development is crucial, as is spotting where, when, and why mistakes are made in learning something new. This opportunity can be lost if a teacher cannot give the individual attention a student may need—or seek. Homework, which diminishes the interaction between teachers and students, goes home with the child, who may struggle with an assignment he or she never quite grasped in the classroom, compounding frustration and often dragging a parent into the quagmire.

Piaget recognized, of course, that not only cognitive development goes through stages. Moral development does so, as well. Though the work of Piaget, Lawrence Kohlberg, and Carol Gilligan differs in important ways, all share a sense that one cannot simply attribute to children the capacity for the kinds of moral reasoning one finds in adults. This recognition that moral reasoning goes through stages has implications for the homework debate.

Criminologists have recently become interested in a phenomenon practiced increasingly widely in our criminal-justice system: trying juvenile offenders in adult courts and subjecting them to the norms and expectations of adult jurisprudence. Defenders of this "tough on youth crime" stance have argued that the young, just like the rest of us, can and must learn to calculate future consequences and delay gratification.

Yet a range of neuropsychological and psychological studies now indicate that in children and young teenagers the messages that are part of such consequentialist reasoning are processed through the amygdala, the prefrontal source of "gut level" pain that provides a context for the more "cerebral" core of the brain. This research has helped explain a phenomenon parents and educators have long noticed in most youngsters and early teenagers–a sense of immortality and an inability to acknowledge distant risks.[10] Such psychological and neurological work would lead one to question the ability of stiff homework assignments for the young to convey the kinds of moral discipline and time-management skills they are supposed to enhance, especially as the rewards connected with homework will be experienced, if at all, only far down the road.

Even Piaget's conception of individualized learning is inadequate in some eyes today. Not only do students progress at different ages, they do not all go through one invariant set of stages. Just as we now recognize that not all students are naturally and appropriately right-handed and should not be made to write in this fashion, we know that distinctive learning styles are developed and may well persist over a whole lifetime. In such a context, the imperative to gear independent projects to the particular limits of the individual child becomes even stronger. Let us consider some scenarios, all drawn from "real-life" teaching situations, that illustrate the limits of homework as a central educational strategy.

Consider a third-grade child having difficulty learning to read. In many schools today, the assumption is that the child needs both to be read to by a parent and to practice reading drills at home to supplement what is happening in the classroom. Unfortunately, under such a scenario the child may often go home to a family in which parents themselves have trouble reading. Or the parent may read but fail to understand the drills or be unable to assist the child in a way he or she can understand. Often exhausted by a school day in which failure has already been frequent, the child now engages in difficult and complicated drills that frustrate both parent and child.

A teenager goes home with the assignment to complete twenty long-division problems. She struggles with the subtraction and multiplication skills necessary to the process and turns in a paper with many wrong answers.

Another teenager is asked to write an essay on the origins and significance of the Electoral College. The essay defines the Electoral College, then meanders into a discussion of the difference between an electoral majority and a popular majority.

In all of these cases, unsatisfactory work is presented in class to the teacher on the following day. But what does the teacher learn from this? In the case of the third-grader, should she or he infer that the child is lazy or that the parent does not care or is illiterate? What we are increasingly learning is that reading recovery with children who, for whatever reason, have experienced difficulty in the early stages of reading is a specialty, and one that requires attentiveness to the individual needs and motivations of the child.

Many children in underfunded schools have difficulty not primarily because of parental motivation or background but because classes are large, children's difficulties not identified quickly, and most important, well-trained reading-recovery specialists who can work with the child individually are not available. Ohanian cites many instances in which even children with the most severe and long-term reading difficulties have not only learned to read but also developed an interest in reading. The key element in their reading recovery was an adult who could adjust both strategies and assignments to the affective interests and particular strengths and limits of the child. Such children, however, often fail and experience intense frustration when their reading is made dependent on parental drills or one-size-fits-all reading assignments for the child or parent.

In less dramatic fashion, the same saga plays out with the older students. When the incorrect long-division solutions are presented in school, the teacher must not only painstakingly observe that the answers are wrong but also look over the work to assess whether the student miscopied the problem, whether errors crept in because he or she misread a number, or whether the student made a subtraction error or has a problem with multiplication. In many cases, this will be hard to determine.

As for the young student who turns in disorganized and incomplete answers in the social-science essay, did she fail to comprehend the reading adequately? Did she have difficulty understanding the question or in outlining and organizing a response?

The same failures, in short, can be the result of breakdowns at many points along the way. Often the student will have trouble seeing or articulating exactly what went wrong. And even when the teacher receives excellent answers to the questions or exercises posed in homework, one cannot always infer success. Teachers cannot be sure who completes students' homework. Did they exchange answers with friends over the phone? Did mom or dad furnish the answers so that everyone could get on with another phase of the evening? Teachers may eventually be able to evaluate who did the work and what the students' strengths and weaknesses are through tests. Nevertheless, invaluable time will be lost in the process, and bad habits or misinformation can become entrenched. In addition, some students who are doing their homework conscientiously will nevertheless test poorly simply because test-taking is not their forte.

Not only can homework go wrong because different students have hard-to-recognize problems at particular aspects of the process. These problems themselves may well spring from differences in the children's learning styles. It is hard to recognize from homework alone where a child is having difficulty; it is even harder to find just why. Mel Levine, a respected pediatrician whose work is having an increasing influence on the teaching profession, has organized current thinking about learning into what he calls neurodevelopment constructs. These include attention, language, memory, neuromotor function, and social cognition. Within each category are subcategories to convey the brain's complexity. These categories interact in different ways in each individual brain to create a unique learning profile. Levine believes that teachers must spend time with their kids to learn just how the student learns.

A feature article on Levine published in 2000 cited the provocative case of "the kid who constantly looks up and down every time he is copying something from the board. . . . An untrained teacher might accuse him of cheating because he is looking at another student's paper . . . or penalize him for not completing his work." But closer work with him might show that he "had short term memory problems. Some solutions: let him work with another kid or give him a copy of what he already needs written down. Above all ... tell him exactly what the problem is."[11]

For Levine and like-minded researchers, neurophysiology is not destiny, but its particular rhythms and eccentricities within the individual must be acknowledged even as they are worked on by particular educational practices. Levine himself is willing to advocate limited amounts of homework in specific circumstances, but his qualifications amount to a critique of the kind and amount of homework most often prescribed today. The parents must be familiar with the particular learning problem of the child and able to work with that child in ways that respond to those difficulties. In addition, Levine clearly recognizes the exhaustion factor for children and completely repudiates the notion that "laziness" explains children's failures in school.[12]

This research also has direct implications for that other standard fallback of the pro-homework camp: homework's contribution to habits of self-discipline and continued learning throughout life. Not only is the claim that homework evokes long-term discipline largely unsupported by extensive empirical work, but also there is reason to believe that many other extracurricular factors in the life of the child and young adult contribute substantially to this virtue. Kathy Seal, co-author of *Motivated Minds: Raising Children to Love Learning*, argues that "when kids play, they are free to experiment and to learn from their experiences without worrying about how well they're performing.... That's important, because research has shown decisively that that when children study because they enjoy it, their learning is deeper, richer and longer-lasting."[13]

Seal's point is strengthened–though not, of course, proved–
by other related work in neurophysiology. Consider a classic experiment with cats. Two groups of kittens were raised
in the dark; each group was then exposed to light, but in var-
ied ways. Each group was exposed to the same visual stimuli, but the kittens in group 1 were allowed to coordinate
their visual experience with olfactory and tactile sensations
as they moved about, whereas those in group 2 were carried
around and exposed to the visual stimuli. When all of the
animals in the study were released into the environment,
members of the two groups reacted in vastly different ways.
Members of group 1 behaved normally, but those in group
2 acted as if they were blind. They bumped into objects and
fell over edges. These experiments, as well as analogous
experiments on humans and other animals, have led many
neuroscientists away from passive and representational
views of mind. As one group of scientists puts it, "This beau-
tiful study supports the enactive view that objects are not
seen by the visual extraction of features but rather by the
visual guidance of action."[14] These scientists in effect call
into question the long-standing portrait of a passive mind
describing and representing a world apart from its actions
in it. The mind is situated in, and co-dependent on, a host of
neural pathways and psychic and biological energies. Disposition is crucial to its work.

Yet this perspective is not a return to the crude sociobiology that was so prevalent in biology and even social science
in the 1980s. That sociobiology purported to have a model
of mind that explained our thoughts, disposition, and even
our culture in terms of underlying and lawlike genetic and
other somatic factors. In the perspective endorsed here, mind
and culture interact with and shape, and are shaped by, the

relays and feedback loops in which they are situated. Many, including myself, would add the further assumption, shared by at least some modern neurophysiologists and philosophers of science, that the natural world in which mind is situated, though far from chaotic, manifests its own periodic bursts of unpredictable agency. That world is not fully describable by causal laws; nor is it bound to realize one underlying purpose. The political theorist William Connolly has nicely summarized this perspective:

> In a way reminiscent of Bergson, Merleau-Ponty, and Hampshire they now emphasize how the practical activities of embodied human beings give priority to know-how over propositional knowledge. They put emphasis on the compositional element of thinking while playing down its representational function. People, of course, do form representations. But these are not neutral representations of a world waiting to be copied. They are operational representations by corporeal agents *engaged* in culturally mediated, practical activities of perceiving, working, playing, deciding, evaluating, and judging in a world that simultaneously responds to these operational representations and *exceeds* them.[15]

Thought itself thus depends in large measure on invoking the active interest and engagement of the individual in the world. The most creative forms of thought often occur at the margins, where established truths and axioms bump up against underlying dispositions and fears that both mediate and challenge those thoughts.

That homework could never be designed in such a way that it evokes a sense of joy from perpetual play amid a world of ultimate indeterminacy is not my contention. But clearly much homework would have to be redesigned in ways that are responsive to individual interests and are buttressed by appropriate supportive physical and emotional environments. But the larger context here is the role of non-academic enrichment in the child's long-term academic advancement. Any educational agenda that fails to leave space and opportunity for such enrichment slights the long-term development and potential creativity of the student-learner.

Many educators are now coming to recognize the importance of offering children and parents various forms of non-academic enrichment on a year-round basis. Karl Alexander, Doris Entwisle, and Linda Olson of Johns Hopkins University point out in their study of children's academic progress that "better off children in the study more often went to city and state parks, fairs, or carnivals and took day or overnight trips. They also took swimming, dance, and music lessons; visited local parks, museums, science centers and zoos; and more often went to the library in summer."[16]

If we take seriously the notion that our cognitive activities are sustained and yet challenged by a natural world in which order and purpose must be constantly re-created against a backdrop of perpetual surprise and challenge, even totally unstructured time may offer other benefits. Some basic concepts, motor and perceptual skills, and basic information is necessary to any civilized life, and schools must convey this information. But even—and perhaps especially—for children, the hours already spent in school amid these necessary pursuits constitute a kind of rat race. And rat races need their limits. I would endorse for children language that Connolly has applied to adult workers: "It is critical that citizens from a variety of walks of life be provided with structural opportunities for periodic retreat from a fast paced life. Such retreats enable us to revisit from time to time selective assumptions and dispositions that have gripped us and to refresh our energies to enter the rat race. In my democratic utopia, for instance, sabbatical leaves would be expanded rather than contracted."[17]

It may well be the case, subversive not only to the political right but also to much of the left, that the importance of play and of totally free time is culturally underappreciated. Not only grade-schoolers but also high-school students and adult workers deserve time for the kind of cultural enrichment and unstructured play that fosters creativity and sustains a life-long interest in learning. Work as the solution to all our woes is reform on the cheap and at the expense of all. Children, like all of us, are more than recipients of school knowledge. They are siblings and community members, budding artists, musicians, and athletes. They are natural inventors and scientists and spiritual beings. Do we allow our children to exercise these selves?

The sporadic local battles over homework in a context in which the issue has not yet achieved the status of a full national debate have led to some curious turns. Not only is there the threat or actuality of failure for those children who do not benefit from parents who can help them through learning experiences that are inappropriate for them, but other parents have found the need to fashion more permanent escapes from the system.

In a recent op-ed piece in the *New York Times*, Arthur Levine (no relation to Mel) points to stunning new trends in American education and draws out what he takes to be their implications. Levine begins by pointing out that a "growing number of America's children are being identified as having learning disabilities." Critics have objected to the unfairness of programs for children with learning disabilities on the grounds that "affluent families are more likely than less wealthy ones to take advantage of accommodations for the learning disabled, like time extensions on standardized tests. And critics charge that mainstreaming of learning disabled students–the trend toward including them in traditional classes–creates disruption."[18]

Levine correctly points out that our current school system was created for an industrial society and resembles an assembly line. "Students are educated by age, in batches of 25 to 30," he writes. "They study for common periods of time, and after completing a specified number of courses, they are awarded diplomas. It is a notion of education dictated by seat time."

Levine goes on to comment prescriptively that, in an information society, the old model of education

> works far less well than it once did. . . . First, our children are diverse in their abilities, so we need a more varied curriculum. Second, because of advances in brain research, we are discovering how individuals actually learn, and this will allow us to develop the educational program each child needs. Third, new technologies that provide different pedagogies and learning materials are burgeoning. We are heading to an era in which schooling will change profoundly. The teacher will not be the talking head at the front of the classroom, but the expert on students' learning styles, the educational equivalent of a medical doctor. Children will no longer be grouped by age. Each student will advance at his or her own pace in each subject area through individual tutorials, student-centered group learning and a cornucopia of new technology and software.

Levine makes a persuasive case that changes in both technology and our understanding of learning will require major educational transformation. I believe that a de-emphasis on homework–at least, in the forms in which it has always been known–is a crucial part of the necessary changes.

Yet Levine may exaggerate the degree to which these insights are new. In varying ways, a range of progressive educators would not have seen his wisdom as utterly foreign. Nevertheless, both he and they might be overemphasizing the role of technology and learning theory in educational reforms. The best insights of the progressive educators could not be implemented largely because those insights carried profound and negative implications for widely held cultural values—values with which an economic and political elite was especially associated. Today, education is at the center of broader value conflicts, and neither learning theory nor technology alone will determine those conflicts' outcome.

2

A History Lesson about
Work and Homework

IN THE PAST THREE YEARS, the theme of family stress, not only for the poor but also for working- and middle-class families, has become a regular staple of media attention. *Time, Newsweek,* and *U.S. News and World Report* all featured cover stories emphasizing the "stressed-out" family and pointing to both work and homework as important components of that stress. These popular magazines describe a familiar litany. Parents come home from long-hour jobs and must then wrestle with homework over the kitchen table. The articles suggest that parents learn how to manage their children's outside activities better and place limits wherever possible on their own work. Nevertheless, by and large, the stresses are seen as endemic to modern high-technology life or as the small, necessary price all human beings must pay for their natural desire for an ever expanding standard of material comfort.

Absent from these magazines is the recognition that most parents have little opportunity to limit their own hours of work. Furthermore, the media treatment is historically my-

opic. God did not dictate hours of work and homework; nor
have they always been the same. Work in all its forms has been
a topic of political discussion at many points not only in our
history but in the history of other modern industrial societies.

Newsweek nicely captured the tone of the current discussion of middle-class life in a cover article characterizing family life as "a triathlon with no finish line in sight.... Their
lives have become a daily frantic rush in the minivan from
school to soccer to piano lessons and then hours of homework." But they are trapped. Parents may at times despair,
but they are "afraid to slow down because any blank space
in the family calendar could mean their offspring won't have
the résumés to earn thick letters from Harvard—and big
bucks forever after." Parents therefore "sacrifice their dwin-
dling free time ... to make sure their kids are safe and want
for nothing.... With stakes so high, parents are pressing for
school to be more challenging, which has resulted in more
homework, more testing."[1]

For these parents, such strategies are choices undertaken
to keep the American dream of success and affluence alive.
As *U.S. News* puts it, one cannot imagine how the glories of
Silicon Valley would have emerged without total commitments to work: "Innovation and demonic commitment tend
to go hand in hand, after all.... America was built on a foundation of hard work as well as natural bounty. As an immigrant nation, the United States benefited from a large pool
of workers self-selected for their long term horizons and
their readiness to endure hardship in the here and now."[2]
Those societies that do choose to limit hours of work through
either government or union actions pay a high price, *U.S.
News* suggests. Any jealousy about their shorter hours "might
be checked by a peek at the recent economic record. Roughly

10 percent unemployment is the norm across much of Western Europe, with its already-successful efforts to reduce working hours."³

In the course of many interviews and debates, I have noticed that it comes as a surprise to many that the practices and policies regarding hours of both work and homework have displayed considerable variation over even the past half-century. Some of the more informed homework advocates now acknowledge that homework has waxed and waned as an educational practice in the twentieth century, but even they fail to recognize or acknowledge the connections homework bears on the practice of and ideals about work in the larger society.

Two related, long-standing cultural tendencies are at play in the homework debate. More than those in any other advanced industrial nation, U.S. business and educational elites have treated work as an all-encompassing, absolute good. Part of that mindset has included blaming the poor's reputed unwillingness to work and inability to defer gratification for poverty.

The salience of homework reflects not merely pedagogical concerns but long-standing battles about how much time parents and children have, how work time is compensated, how time is conceived, and who controls that time. E. P. Thompson pointed out that, in many rural, "pre-industrial" societies, time is not clock or sidereal time. Time is understood in terms of the daily or seasonal rhythms of life, harvests, and the ebb and flow of the tides. Workers modulated their days in terms of the seasonal demands of the harvest. Work was part of a shared community life and was seen as an expression of and means toward the common relations of the community. Workers came and went through the day, trading stories and following their own pace.⁴

With the emergence of the modern corporation and the broader ethos of industrial capitalism, however, time in the sense of clock time in its measured, invariant pattern had to take on more significance. More sophisticated and accurate clocks, themselves the products of industrial economies, oversaw the reorganization of a society now oriented toward viewing nature–and time–as resources to be controlled and mined in pursuit of ever greater productivity. In the British context, where the emerging factory system was controlled by individual owners, these owners were no longer willing to tolerate milling about. Workers lost control of their time at work. They then demanded that their working hours be limited so they would enjoy time outside the workplace.

Many aspects of this historic struggle are instructive. A major goal of many labor groups in the nineteenth century was to shorten the hours of work, with eight hours a day, six days a week being the target. Though some modern historians have attributed primarily economic motives to this struggle (shorter hours are one way to tighten labor markets and increase wages), economics appears to have been only one motive. Benjamin Kline Hunnicutt, the leading historian of leisure, points out that for the new social historians,

> leisure ... permitted the expression of traditional values and customs, the formation of class consciousness, and the maintenance of institutions such as family, church, and community. Thus leisure has been seen as important because it was necessary for the expression of a whole category of nonpecuniary motives.... In addition, several historians have shown that many workers did not accept the dominant work ethic, and in their time away from the job they found supportive social contexts in which to express alternative values.[5]

Herbert Gutman's work on industrializing America suggests that instilling the work ethic was also a matter of stigmatizing and ultimately sanctioning that which was seen as contrary to it, or was even intensified in reaction to it. Holidays, religious rituals, and weekend social events involving wine or spirits were all subject to bitter attack.[6] Firms lengthened working days and tried to instill the importance of work. For many pre-industrial communities, wine had been a part of the normal routines of family and work life. Once placed within the factory regime, the struggle between workers and employers often led to set breaks for these forms of recreation, but then eventually to their definition as forms of deviance. They were harshly repressed even when there appear to have been no grounds for suspecting they impeded workers' safety. They were simply part of, and helped symbolize, a way of life in which work and its rewards were not the central theme.

Even as far back as Britain in the eighteenth century, schools were playing a major role in struggles over time and the work ethic. Complaining that idle and ragged children were clogging the streets of Manchester, failing to use their time and engaged in gambling, one moralist praised charity schools for teaching "Industry, Frugality, Order and Regularity." Children as young as four were to be sent to workhouses, where they would work and be schooled two hours a day. The aim was to see that the child was "constantly employed at least twelve hours a day, whether they earn their living or not; for by those means, we hope that the rising generation will be so habituated to constant employment that it would at length prove agreeable and entertaining to them."[7]

In the United States, a major concern of the late–nineteenth-century common-school movement was to bring youngsters into the school system to instill attitudes about time, work, and punctuality that would counteract what were seen as the doleful effects of immigrant working-class culture. By the late nineteenth century, the National Association of Manufacturers was equating leisure with "crime, vice, the waste of man's natural capacity, corruption, radicalism, debt, decay, degeneration, and decline."[8] Not only were law and political repression one appropriate response, but industry proposed a velvet glove as well. Schools were seen as "the balance wheel of society." Schools especially could teach the habits of prompt obedience.[9]

By the late nineteenth century, a majority of Americans had migrated from farm to city, and many worked very long hours in factories. Children, too, were caught up in this process. With parents strapped for both time and money, the labor of the child, in the home or in the workplace, was often desperately needed.

Family life centered on work. For many immigrants from pre-industrial cultures, the school played a central role in disciplining students to the long working hours and consumption habits of an expanding market economy. Nevertheless, regardless of whether school detracted from time for household labor or sent a message regarding industrial work and consumption that many immigrant parents did not want to hear, the relationship between school and many working-class parents was conflictual. As they do today, parents undoubtedly complained about all the work their children were asked to do at school. Parents then often complained that homework caused ill health because students did not have a chance to play in fresh air and sunshine, both thought to be key ingredients for good health.

Just as there were ongoing movements to limit working hours, there were movements to limit homework during this period. Concerns about the health risks of over-studying led some schools to limit or abolish homework altogether.[10] School principals, often heavily influenced by business and professional leaders committed to the culture of work, were reluctant to accept parental demands to limit homework. They reasoned that, because parents had the option to send their children to school, those who wished to do so must be willing to abide by the schools' rules. They argued that homework was not harmful to health and that it was an essential pedagogical tool. Without broad-based support from school personnel, anti-homework movements of the nineteenth century had little long-lasting effect.

By the end of the century, however, public sentiment began to change, and the pressure on the schools to abolish homework mounted. Homework was on the national agenda. In the 1880s, the president of the Boston school board, Francis A. Walker, a widely respected Civil War hero, strongly criticized the practice:

> Over and over again have I had to send my own children, in spite of their tears and remonstrances, to bed, long after the assigned tasks had ceased to have any educational value and had become the means of nervous exhaustion and agitation, highly prejudicial to body and to mind; and I have no reason to doubt that such has been the experience of a large proportion of the parents whose children are habitually assigned home lessons in arithmetic.[11]

This anti-homework sentiment focused on two key issues. One was that of whether there was in fact any educational value in homework. The other was homework's perceived threat to the physical, emotional, and mental health of the child. For advocates of children's emotional health, even arguments as to its perceived educational value were outweighed by its long-term damage to the child.

The turn-of-the-century anti-homework crusade became a centerpiece in the agenda of the progressive education movement of the twentieth century. Educational leaders began to question the very structure of teaching in the schools. In questioning the value of drills, memorization, and recitation, the attendant need for homework came under harsh scrutiny.[12]

The First Half of the Twentieth Century: Health and Happiness

It is probably hard for us to read this account of the homework debates in the first half of the twentieth century without wondering what it would be like to have lived then. Imagine taking your child to the eye doctor for glasses and having the doctor write a letter advising the school that the child should do no more homework because it is bad for her eyes. Or instead of prescribing Ritalin for your ten-year-old son, the doctor prescribes seven hours of vigorous physical exercise—*before* school each day. Or instead of labeling your child as having attention deficit hyperactivity disorder (ADHD), a doctor testifies at a school-board meeting that homework is driving your child into a nervous condition.

While educational leaders began to question the practice in their circles, parents who struggled with their children over homework could find solace in the writings of Edward Bok, editor of the *Ladies' Home Journal*. His 1900 article "A National Crime at the Feet of American Parents" sounded the rallying cry for the anti-homework forces.[13] In the article, he argued that homework brought grave health risks. He cited a lack of sunshine and fresh air as a leading cause of the nervous disorders from which thousands of young people suffered. He pointed out that "five hours a day of brain work [is] the most we should ask of our children." He stated that schooling had changed so much in the previous ten years that parents could not be expected to help their children with schoolwork. He asked that homework be abolished for children younger than fifteen and that it be limited to an hour a night for older children. He called on parents to take the lead in bringing schools and parents together and asked that parents demand of their schools new limits on homework.

In numerous *Ladies' Home Journal* articles Bok built the case that homework was an intrusion on family life and that it interfered with the rights of children and parents.[14] Physicians, arguing forcefully about the health risks of homework, joined the battle.

Bok's writing helped galvanize a more widespread movement. By 1930, the Society for the Abolition of Homework had been organized. By then, progressive ideas had taken hold in education.[15] Increasingly, schools were viewed as the workplace of the young. In the best Progressive tradition, these workplaces were often seen as in need of reforms that would guarantee humane conditions for workers. And the role of the expert was paramount. The work of the school must be done in the school, under the watchful eye of the trained teacher and in the specially designed environment of the school. Educators came to see the educational importance of lighting, the size and shape of desks, and quiet spaces. They argued that few homes offered this environment and therefore were ill suited for studying.[16] Just as basically, progressive educators were concerned that schools treat and educate the child as an individual, a task best carried out through direct interaction of the educator and the child.

These educators provided an important critique of and response to traditional educational goals. Reflecting, and in turn helping to shape, concerns and goals widely shared by the labor movement, progressive educators responded to the growing industrial prosperity of the 1920s by asking a fundamental question: to what purposes will society place increasing productivity and prosperity? Educators throughout most of the nineteenth century, just like most educational leaders today, had assumed that the purpose of education was to prepare future workers for their jobs in an economy in which hard work was the only way to meet basic survival needs.

By the 1920s, however, many progressive educators believed that growing prosperity and productivity offered at least two significantly different possibilities for the future course of capitalist workplaces and schools. Generalized prosperity meant that the demands for future consumption could be lessened. In addition, with declining emphasis on production and consumption, the number of hours spent at work could and would diminish.

The 1920s are often portrayed in standard history texts as an era of conservative consensus. At the level of national politics, this judgment is sound. Nevertheless, within education circles a fundamental struggle was occurring between industrial capitalist responses to increased prosperity and those of many reform educators. For many industrial leaders, ever increasing prosperity became as much a threat as an opportunity. If productivity made consumer satiation possible, overcapacity and eventual economic decline might result. Or at the very least, the role and significance of the business leader within the economy and society would be diminished. In part as a response to these trends and concerns, business leaders articulated a set of purposes and practices characterized as the "gospel of consumption." This gospel pictured human beings as essentially acquisitive and work as the key to the ever increasing wages and salaries needed to sustain acquisitiveness. Institutionally, the role of advertising and consumer credit as stimulants and mechanisms of consumption grew dramatically in this decade.

As Hunnicutt has pointed out, educators "actively competed with business and industry for control of the time freed by economic abundance."[17] Many argued strenuously against the notion that the purpose of education should be limited to job creation. Their reasoning was that jobs themselves would soon be requiring less time from U.S. workers and that the skills needed for such jobs could be acquired in a relatively short period within the workplace itself.

The task of education thus must become fundamentally different. Americans "could be prepared for the 'worthy' use of leisure through proper education and could be prevented from converting to the gospel of consumption."[18] Education for the worthy use of leisure took on so much importance in the 1920s that it became one of the National Education Association's cardinal principles of education, often totally eclipsing the others in the attention it received.

The "worthy use of leisure" is of course a term suspended in ambiguity. Such a goal could dictate the replacement of a materialistic gospel by another theistically imposed or inspired one. Nevertheless, although some late–nineteenth-century reformers had seen public recreational facilities primarily as tools to socialize, or "Americanize," immigrant children, the vision of cultural enhancement endorsed by 1920s leaders was more democratic and individualistic. A key feature of education was to be education in the arts and humanities with the goal of giving students increased capacity for and interest in individual artistic expression. As Hunnicutt puts it: "Supporters and teachers of liberal arts courses and traditional curriculum offerings thought that by making the masses proficient in the humanities, in those regions of the intellect and imagination that made life full, they could transform the barren space in workers' lives into a fertile ground for democratic culture and creative individuals."[19]

Inspired in part by national battles being waged by labor leaders over working conditions and work hours, some school reformers attacked homework as an illicit extension of the working day. These critics wanted to apply the newly defined child labor laws to schoolwork. To them, homework was work and should be regulated as such.[20]

These critics' central concern was the health risks of homework. Homework was believed to be the cause of eye strain, stress, inadequate sleep, and deformity. The writer of a 1935 letter to the *New York Times* claimed that "homework is directly responsible for more undernourished, nervous, bespectacled, round-shouldered children than you can possibly imagine."[21] As part and parcel of the health argument against homework, many regretted children's loss of an important element of childhood–play. Just as some psychologists and labor advocates in the 1920s and '30s began to cite the role of recreation in human development during their campaigns to shorten the workweek, educational reformers argued that play was an integral part of the development of the child. Homework was seen as limiting the child's ability to develop the skills and attitudes that can be learned only when the child is free to play. One educator of the day argued that children at age ten needed six or seven hours of vigorous physical activity daily.[22]

War, Work, and Homework

Concerns about the downsides of work and homework reached a peak during the Great Depression in the 1930s. Rank-and-file unionists and even many members of Congress pushed for passage of the Black-Connery bill, which would have mandated a thirty-hour work week. After initial support, the Roosevelt administration reversed gears and put its energy into labor-reform legislation that would lay out fair labor standards and a federally controlled system to monitor the process of workplace unionization.

The New Deal liberals' retreat had long-term implications not merely for labor unions and workers, but also ultimately for many families with children. As opposed as many businesses were to unions, large corporations were far more willing to work with unions than with dramatic reductions in hours of work. Even during an era of labor glut, control over working hours remained a sacred prerogative in the eyes of many business leaders.

Labor for its part made a major shift in gears. To gain a position that was ideologically more palatable, and in response to the harsh reality of unemployment, labor leaders defended Black-Connery primarily as an economic strategy. Shortening hours would create more jobs for the unemployed.

However much such a stance helped in securing the Fair Labor Standards Act of 1938, it served over the long term to remove some of labor's momentum on working hours. Once the goal of hours policy was seen as full employment, gains in employment seemed to lessen its rationale.

World War II both capped the process and added two further supports for work. War led to the cultural valorization of work and effort in the struggle first against the Nazis, and then in the incipient Cold War. Once fighting men returned from the war, they largely displaced women in factories and labor unions, voices that had been especially interested in the qualitative dimensions of hours reduction.

Though the widespread push to limit working hours came to an end after World War II, the movement had enduring significance. For more than a century, the number of hours worked declined steadily. And even as labor lost the fight to further limit working hours after World War II, business leaders made major concessions on other fronts to ensure their control of time. Forty hours was established as a standard, and even as it has been frequently exceeded in the past two decades, compensation at time and a half overtime has improved material standards of living.

Thus, homework advocates such as Janine Bempechat who argue that today's working- and middle-class Americans would not "be living in the homes in which they live and the communities in which they settled had they not worked very hard to educate themselves"[23] are providing a one-sided portrait of immigrant and working-class life. Many immigrant families had more time to spend with their children, as well as more prosperous and earlier retirements, because of political struggles to limit hours of work.

Unfortunately, much of the second half of the twentieth century saw repeated endeavors to intensify both work and homework. *Sputnik* is perhaps the best-known marker of a sea change in attitudes toward work and homework, but its significance can be traced to deeper transformations and tensions in the culture. In 1957, the popular media told us that the Soviets had "beaten" us into space with the 1957 launch of *Sputnik*. That event became a catalyst or excuse for major long-term changes in the educational landscape.

Suddenly, the fifty-year trend toward less homework came to an end, and the country became obsessed with competing with the Soviet Union. Homework was portrayed as a key element in the competition. Admiral Hyman Rickover, the father of the nuclear navy, made a career of ridiculing U.S. schools. As Gerald Bracey has commented, Rickover "looked at European schools and without a lot of evidence declared them more rigorous than our own."[24] Striving to make the point stick, Rickover warned: "Let us never forget that there can be no second place in a contest with Russia and that there will be no second chance if we lose." In March 1958, *Life* magazine published a five-part series titled "Crisis in Education," which prominently contrasted a stern-faced Russian student conducting optics experiments in his school lab with a happy-go-lucky American. A large photo shows the American boy laughing as he returns to his seat after "struggling" with a geometry problem at the blackboard. Such stories had an immense impact on popular sensibilities, and for the next few years the vast majority of educators and parents were in favor of more homework.

Coming as it did just a year after the launch of *Sputnik*, the National Defense Education Act (NDEA) sought to strengthen math and science education. It provided loans to undergraduates and fellowships to graduate students. Guidance and testing services were to be overhauled and curricula revised and strengthened. Requiring students to do more math homework was a major cultural and curricular emphasis.

It is, of course, easy to view this emphasis on more math and science at home and in school as appropriate responses to an international emergency. But as we look back on this adventure, some questions should come to mind. Whatever the failings of American schools, by the early 1960s the

United States had clearly established its pre-eminence in the space race. It is hard to assume that any changes in public education enacted in those four or five years could have suddenly given the nation the crop of highly trained engineers it needed to advance the space program. One might suspect that the United States was not really behind in the space race, and, as even many John F. Kennedy loyalists have since admitted, the 1960 campaign talk of a missile gap was manufactured for political purposes.

Surely continued Soviet development of missiles and satellite technology constituted a potential long-term threat to the United States. Nevertheless, many other indicators of military might were widely employed by military analysts. In all these areas, the United States was universally deemed superior. Why did so many political and media leaders focus so intently on this one event and use it primarily as a way to strengthen conventional commitments to and beliefs in the sanctity of homework, especially work focused on technological development and expansion?

The explanation lies not only in the dynamics of international politics and the Cold War but also in broader questions of national identity.[25] At the level of Cold War politics, the Eisenhower administration knew, based on its own high-altitude surveillance of the Soviets, that the United States retained, as it had throughout the Cold War, an overwhelming advantage in missile-delivery technology. Nevertheless, it was unwilling to divulge publicly its aerial photographs and thereby invite Soviet protest. U.S. leaders felt it was important to convey an image of absolute moral rectitude in its dealings with foreign states, even though they knew such an image was false in many ways. The Eisenhower administration was caught in a vise of its own making. It could not present its most conclusive evidence of U.S. military superiority.

Sputnik also became an occasion to repress or counter other broader doubt, cultural controversies, and anxieties. Several regional and cultural phenomena disturbed political elites as well as ordinary citizens in the era leading up to *Sputnik,* including: 1) The September 1957 crisis in race relations, culminating in the forced desegregation of public schools in Little Rock, Arkansas; 2) the decolonization and occasional leftward moves of some African nations; and 3) the rise of a counterculture that presumed but also questioned the fruits of affluence. These phenomena reflected a nation unsure about the centrality, inclusiveness, or complete truth of its guiding ideals of free enterprise and economic growth.

Throughout the late 1950s and early '60s, a major goal of U.S. cultural and political elites was not merely to repel territorial threats to the United States but also to contain domestic challenges to mainstream cultural norms. In this regard, it is instructive to re-examine just how selective U.S. elites were in the lessons they drew from the Soviet threat. The Soviets, by virtue of the success demonstrated by *Sputnik,* were viewed as poised to, and able to, destroy us. Yet no one concluded from this purported fact that the United States should copy the Soviets' relatively more meritocratic educational system or engage in its processes of economic planning with a focus on long-term heavy-industrial development. Portraying a "collectivist" economic system as eager to destroy us, business and political leaders reaffirmed and rallied support for conventional U.S. values of individual initiative, hard work, corporate enterprise, and technological advance. The invocation of *Sputnik* was hardly intended to address schools alone. As one business group worried aloud, "Will the Soviets cut *their* overtime?"[26]

By working hard in schools, labs, and workplaces, we could achieve far more success than the Soviets and set an example the "Third World" would admire. Facing a common enemy, U.S. citizens were encouraged to put racial divisiveness behind them so that the rest of the world would embrace American values.

The urge to see the value of work, economic growth, and individual initiative as final and all-encompassing carried with it the imperative to put aside any inner doubts. What better way than to regard and portray all that differs from the prevalent culture as not merely different but also as the consequence of contamination from foreign influence and thereby dangerous?

The focus on work, homework, math, and science, driven as much by cultural insecurities and an obsession to affirm traditional values as by any documented foreign military challenge, took a major toll. It displaced a whole set of questions that deserved more attention at the time. The failure to address such questions would have implications for a series of foreign and domestic crises the U.S. would face from the late 1960s on. Questions that might have been addressed included the following: If NDEA does improve math and science learning in schools and homes, would our business and government leaders make the best use of newly trained students? Were there other demands implicit in our business and consumer culture that led some students here and many abroad to resist the "American way of life"? Even if the United States were to retain and increase its lead as the predominant military and economic power, would that example itself carry all before it? And, did the United States need unanimity of purposes and lifestyles to retain the allegiance of its citizens and an ability to survive?

By the 1960s, homework had come to be seen as a means for increasing academic achievement, even though the research to prove this claim was just as problematic then as now. In reaction to increased attention to the importance of homework, a homework debate in the late 1960s and '70s echoed the concerns raised in the early part of the century. Once again, this debate reflected and reinforced other concerns about the whole political economy. As such late 1960s classics as Studs Terkel's *Working* suggested, many American workers, not simply disaffected college students, were concerned about the pace and length of the working day as well as the quality of life in the workplace.

In an analogous way, newspapers and women's magazines suggested that children were too tired to do homework. Parents argued that children worked a full day at school and should, like any worker, be free at night to engage in leisure-time activities. Parents felt that homework disrupted family life and caused tensions between them and their children. Some worried that homework reduced interest and enthusiasm for school. Others were concerned that homes were not conducive to study and that homework stunted development. This time around, mental health workers worried about suicide and questioned whether school pressure was part of the problem. A statement by the American Educational Research Association emphasizes the concern:

> For mental health, children and young people need to engage in worthwhile out-of-school tasks suited to their individual capacities. Homework should supply such tasks and reasonable freedom in carrying them out. Whenever homework crowds out social experience, outdoor recreation, and creative activities, and whenever it usurps time that should be devoted to sleep, it is not meeting the basic needs of children and adolescents.[27]

The National Education Association took up the cause by issuing its own statement in 1966:

> It is generally recommended (a) that children in the early elementary school period have no homework specifically assigned by the teacher; (b) that limited amounts of home-work—not more than an hour a day—be introduced during the upper elementary school and junior high years; (c) that homework be limited to four nights a week; and (d) that in secondary school no more than one and a half hours a night be expected. If the weekends and one evening in the middle of the week are left free, the pupil has the opportunity to develop appreciation and skill in art and music and participate more fully in the social life of the family and community. The trend, theoretically at least, is toward homework that is optional, creative, and recreational.[28]

The battle over homework was strongest during the 1930s and 1960s, two progressive periods in our political and educational history. Furthermore, these progressive currents in educational discourse resonated with other debates of those periods. Labor leaders, cultural critics, and many reformers questioned whether the amount of time spent in both homework and factory work was detrimental to the physical health and creativity of students and workers. Today many educators label these two periods in educational history as romantic or sentimental. In this respect, they mirror mainstream business and political resistance to economic reform of all kinds.

Progressive educators believed that schools needed to educate the whole child and that a happy, joyful child is an essential condition for education. Parents of the day were also the beneficiaries of these progressive beliefs. Homework was seen as unfair to parents, who worked hard all day and deserved some rest and relaxation at home without the strain of homework.

Homework and a "Nation at Risk"

As the United States entered the 1980s, education reform was once again a key theme. As in the post-*Sputnik* era, the language was of foreign challenge and the rhetoric was militaristic. But now, the terrain was the economy and the risks were viewed as the loss of our capacity for economic survival. The 1983 report *A Nation at Risk* to this day defines the landscape for our debates about education.

The authors of that report suggest: "Our Nation is at risk. Our once unchallenged preeminence in commerce, industry, science, and technological innovation is being overtaken by competitors throughout the world. . . . If an unfriendly power had attempted to impose on America the mediocre educational performance that exists today, we might well have viewed it as an act of war."[29] In the course of a general commentary on U.S. education, the authors go on to emphasize higher standards in math, science, English, and foreign-language instruction. They argue that homework has been too diminished and that students need to do more homework and work a much longer school year.

Ostensibly, the tone and recommendations of this document can be attributed to the growing success being enjoyed at the time by the Japanese. The United States was experiencing not only relatively slow economic growth but also a deepening balance-of-trade deficit with Japan. Nevertheless, just as the backdrop for *Sputnik* was a set of doubts and conflicts over economic growth, racial justice, the role of the United States in a decolonizing world, *A Nation at Risk* was written with late-1970s concerns and anxieties as its subtext.

For many Americans, the role of economic growth as the key to the good life was balanced by concerns that unlimited growth might be doing irreparable damage to the planet. For others, the relentless emphasis on work and consumption disrupted family life and eroded leisure activities. These implicit challenges to, or anxieties regarding, central values were hardly acknowledged in *A Nation at Risk*. Not only was the ethic of individual initiative, hard work, and production portrayed as central to our survival, but other nations with divergent values and practices were seen as uniquely bent on our destruction and willing to stop at nothing to achieve that end. Thus, Japanese practices of subsidizing strategic industries are noted briefly, but no mention was made of the role that subsidies and tariffs played in this nation's own economic development. Foreign economic systems are portrayed as completely different from ours and utterly hostile to us:

> History is not kind to idlers. The time is long past when American destiny was assured simply by an abundance of inexhaustible human enthusiasm and by our relative isolation from the malignant problems of older civilization. The world is indeed one global village. We live among determined, well educated, and strongly motivated competitors. We compete with them for international standing and markets, not only with products but also with the ideas of our laboratories and neighborhood workshops. America's position in the world may once have been reasonably secure with only a few exceptionally well-trained men and women. It is no longer.

Once again, as with the *Sputnik* controversy, the authors of *A Nation at Risk* left unexamined the role that a whole set of established American institutions may have played in whatever economic dislocations were being experienced. Jobs were being "lost" to Japanese competitors, but no mention was made of American firms that "moved" those jobs or totally relocated. Education was portrayed as a vehicle for

establishing and reinforcing common values, but not for
challenging received wisdom or redressing social inequities.
Finally, in language that has become virtually canonic today,
the globalization of commerce and the "global village" were
taken simply as a given, with no mention of the political,
institutional, and technological choices that had gone into
their creation.

In such a context, it is not surprising that the authors
endorsed longer homework hours. It fits well with established notions of individualism and an emphasis on work as
the central feature of life. Nor does it lead to questioning of
the opportunities workers have, or roles they actually play,
in major U.S. corporations.

The push for homework has indeed waxed and waned
throughout our history. One can portray homework as a necessary and salutary response to external demands on our
political economy. From such a perspective, homework
would be unexceptional, like the kind of training a marathon
runner must do to meet the biological challenge of running
the race. But societies are more than passive receptors, and
external events not only are understood but are also recognized only though categories that help us make sense of our
experience.

To the extent our leaders are bent on confirming a view
of work, economic growth, individual initiative, and market
economies as not only reasonable ways to organize life but
as the only way, they are likely to portray gripes about homework as little more than the loneliness of the long-distance
runner. But if there are reasons to doubt both the centrality
and the all-inclusive nature of such values, homework is
worth a second look.

Homework is on center stage once again. The challenge posed, militarily or ideologically, by the Soviets has been replaced by the more diffuse but equally problematic rhetoric of global trade wars. By the 1990s, politicians were calling from the halls of Congress for more homework. In the 1994 State of the Union address, President Bill Clinton encouraged parents to help their children with their homework. Homework hotlines, Internet nodes, and high-price tutors have all sprung up to meet the increasing demands of homework. Homework has once again been integrated into debates about work life and more broadly the very sanctity of our way of life. But unlike the 1930s and the 1960s, these efforts clearly reflect an endeavor by business and political leaders to impart and defend their view of the political economy.

The Contemporary Politics of Work, Homework, and Consumption

Business executives routinely celebrate homework today. Even if homework fails to produce smarter workers, it does help acclimatize them to what corporations want now: workers who are used to, and will not complain about, the long working day. One *Fortune*-500 CEO, asked by Juliet Schor to comment on the possibility of a shorter workweek, responded in the following very telling language: "My view of the world, our country, and our country's needs is diametrically opposite of yours. I cannot imagine a shorter workweek. I can imagine a longer one both in school and at work if America is to be competitive in the first half of the next century."[30] A workforce accustomed to some free time during its formative years, by contrast, is a political force more likely to suggest that issues of free time are every bit as important an economic good as more goods and services.

Nevertheless, this celebration of homework is as strident as it is in part because it is challenged on some outposts today. There is already evidence to suggest that time within the workplace and time spent on homework are growing cultural concerns. One indication of just how significant these concerns are is the effort by mainstream media to play them down, either through casual hints that American children do not work too much or by saying that Americans may work hard, but this is the price they pay for the rich life in terms of consumer goods for which they naturally lust. But these rejoinders suggest a further need for an ecumenical politics if homework and workplace reform are to succeed.

The argument that Americans want to consume ever more goods and services must be addressed frontally by education reformers today, just as their predecessors needed to address and critique the gospel of consumption in the 1920s. Consumption patterns have implications for educational and economic reform. Furthermore, such discussions allow labor reformers and educators to initiate dialogue with the growing environmental movement. For this contact to be fruitful, the dialogue should be informed by a politics of consumption, one that shared with many environmentalists concerns about consumption but that questioned the sacrosanct notion—even among many environmentalists—that consumption is simply a "natural" human preoccupation that can or must be disciplined by external restraint.

Schor has properly pointed to the role that a "work-and-spend" cycle plays in this dynamic.[31] That cycle is the historic residue of the struggles over work, homework, and leisure discussed earlier in this chapter. Most modern workers seldom have control over the number of hours spent in the workplace. At best, they gain increasing wages as the productivity of workplaces improves. They could save these wages and hope eventually to escape the workplace, but such a course would require many years.

In any case, there are also immense social pressures to spend increased incomes. These include the peer pressures of the workplace itself. Citizens now spend more of their waking hours at work or engaged in work than in any other venue. Income disparities within those workplaces have grown dramatically. Can one hope to go up the corporate ladder—or even retain one's job—if one fails to embrace the lifestyle of the most successful? Consumption in short becomes a way to achieve both personal identity and a sense of social connectedness. Unfortunately, it is a very unstable ground, as the ante is always being upped, and the social and environmental consequences are substantial.

Paradoxically, the very emphasis on work, wages, and consumption, sanctioned formally and informally within our political economy, also undermine other forms of community and self-expression. We come to enjoy little opportunity for recreation, community events, local politics, and family life. Our diminished opportunities in this regard in turn reinforce the reliance on wages and the workplace.

Schor's analysis of market capitalism and her reflections on labor history have important implications for the home work debate. One consequence of an economy with substantial unemployment is that employers have the power not only to deskill jobs but also to lengthen the hours of these jobs. These strategies go together. Long-hour jobs serve the interests of the employer because they minimize net training costs and create a pool of unemployed workers willing to take the job. That pool of unemployed workers makes it harder for the employed to protest the conditions of their employment.

Schor identifies some further pressures that lead to the intensification of the work-and-spend cycle, pressure on children to work long hours, and the desertion of the public sector as an appropriate vehicle for resolving these problems.

Schor's fundamental premise is that we are social beings. We are lost without some set of socially constructed norms to guide us. In a society in which some version of the Protestant work ethic has always valorized work and material success as its just rewards, getting and spending have added meaning to life. Consumer goods–especially the ones that are visible–are statements about ourselves. More to the point, they often have also been an expression of one's individuality, a distinctly American phenomenon.

But if social and personal identity are necessary, must the identity be regarded as forever unalterable, subject to neither contestation nor limits? By implication, Schor argues that an identity of getting and spending has taken a social toll at least as severe as its environmental toll and that challenges and limits to this identity are possible.

The identity constituted by working, getting, and spending can be a trap as much as it is a support. Any identity can bring about doubts and forms of personal or collective resistance. Perhaps the best forms of identity are those that also acknowledge possible limits and invite debate. Unfortunately, this is just what a work- and consumer-oriented society has most resisted in recent years.

In the 1950s and 1960s, consumerism may have given rise to the kind of bland and occasionally oppressive conformity symbolized by Levittown, but the standards were often set as much by neighbors as by distant authority. In neighborhoods in which income ranges were relatively small, many could meet the standards.

Today's consumerism is qualitatively far more problematic. The role of the neighborhood in our lives is much less substantial. Even in two-parent families, mom is ever less likely to be at home. Mom and dad are both working, and the Joneses with whom they hope to keep up are co-workers and supervisors. For almost everyone, television, with its ads and opulent lifestyles, is the new neighborhood.

In the modern workplace, the power and income spread has reached unprecedented levels. Keeping up appearances is a daunting task. Schor demonstrates, through studies of purchasing patterns for readily identifiable cosmetics and branded clothing and consumer surveys, that much personal spending is designed to position ourselves in an increasingly stratified and competitive universe.

Far from breeding a sense of satisfaction, this new consumerism seems increasingly to disappoint. Much of what we buy we hardly use and often discard. And not surprisingly, keeping up with the higher-ups at work requires endless new consumption. Even as some of us gradually gain the material level to which we aspire, others have also, and the bar is then raised. An obsession to spend ever more often sets in even while many despair of where their lives are going. More than a quarter of those earning more than $100,000 report that they would need very large increases in income just to meet their "needs."

Schor reports that these obsessions with consumer goods have contradictory effects on children, but ones that are well within the framework I have been elaborating. For some children, the impact of their parents' concerns with conspicuous consumption is a continual urge to shop, often to the point that parents worry about the effects of shopping on homework time. But for other kids, homework becomes a vehicle to get ahead so that one can be sure to have enough income to be able to do what their parents either are doing or want to do.

Paradoxically, whether kids are pointed toward immediate shopping or toward compulsive workaholism, consumerism is ultimately served. Schools emphasizing long hours of homework, competitive grading, and success on standardized testing fail to nurture intrinsic interests in learning for its own sake. Ohanian has recently illustrated how the pressures of the imperatives of the modern classroom kill an intrinsic interest in learning and sustain consumerism at the same time. In a bid advertised as a way to enhance interest in reading, Pizza Hut inaugurated a reading-incentive program for students, rewarding them with free pizzas for specified amounts of extra reading. In an interview with a critical *New York Times* reporter, Ohanian said:

> I tried to explain that I worked hard at helping my students come to the love of reading for reading's sake, not for the sake of a . . . pizza. . . . I explained that in my classroom when a child finishes reading a book, his reward is to read another book. I tried to explain that if we hope to educate our children, to help them develop good character traits, help them develop autonomy, persistence, and judgment, then we must help them savor learning for its own sake, not just because someone is keeping a scorecard and handing out trophies.[32]

School policies that emphasize reading specific books as part of mandatory homework and then grade this work leave students with few opportunities to develop alternative interests—even a sustained interest in reading. Education inevitably becomes more closely associated with the grades and the eventual income it can yield. A sustained interest in reading is far more likely if kids are encouraged to read what they like to read. But it is just this ability to find and nurture interests outside grades, incomes, and consumption that our economic and educational institutions discourage.

The obsession to spend more on consumer goods also denudes the public sector. In language reminiscent of Rousseau, Schor portrays a world in which extreme individualism and massive inequalities eviscerate political life. As taxes are cut and individuals pour ever more resources into private solutions to their problems, public functions are performed ever less well. The demand for private schools, gated communities, and more highways grows apace.

Keeping up in the consumption game is continually harder to do. At the same time, the costs of not keeping up have increased for many. The insecurities that have marked blue-collar work for a generation now increasingly infect the middle- and upper-management levels, as well. Building on Barbara Ehrenreich's *Fear of Falling*, Schor comments that, for a frightened and squeezed middle class, securing a place means going upscale. How one is perceived may well have a bearing on whether one is a victim of the next downsizing. In workplaces dominated by class differences and class antagonisms, showing that one identifies with the values of the corporation and its owners is just as vital as one's immediate work performance. What better way to demonstrate those values than through one's upscale consumer choices? As Schor notes, "The penalties of dropping down are perhaps the most powerful psychological hooks that keep us keeping up, even as the heights get dizzying."[33]

Schor's analysis of the subtle coercion inside much modern consumerism has provided one more reason that workplace reform should be a priority not only for most workers but for environmentalists, children's advocates, and women enslaved to the second shift. Reducing the massive inequalities in reward and the disparities in power between front-line workers and top-level management and owners would not necessarily end all the emulative consumption. Nevertheless, it would create better conditions to discuss both its causes and effects. When workers enjoy more equitable pay, more input in day-to-day affairs, and a voice in the selection of their own supervisors, the criteria for advancement might be more related to the ability to perform and work with others than to one's choice of power suits or Rolex watches. And where values and identities can be questioned rather than merely imposed, those norms can be held less defensively, and sensible limits can be placed on their reach and grasp.

The very lack of such power in our working lives often commits us to patterns of work and consumption we would not choose if we had alternatives. The growing concern about the harried quality of life and the lack of time for family activities suggests that these worries are hardly matters for progressive intellectuals alone. But these concerns suggest a positive spin, as well. If the lack of workplace power has resulted not only in diminished wages but also in overworked Americans, a progressive movement able and willing to resurrect these concerns has some prospect of success.

Nothing in the perspective developed by Schor is hostile to materialism across the board or dedicated to forcing citizens never to spend on any item not necessary for immediate survival. Indeed, Schor quotes with obvious approval a reformed "shop-aholic" who acknowledges that new and distinctive clothing choices will always remain some part of her reformed life: "I think it's fun to dress . . . but I like to do it on my own terms, not because of pressure to look a certain way."[34]

The world envisioned by Schor is one marked by a far higher degree of political and economic freedom than we now experience. Individuals would have far more choice as to how much they work and spend. They could have the opportunity to carve out personal and social visions that gripped them and yet did not overwhelm and dominate every aspect of their waking lives. If consumerism teaches a cautionary lesson, it is that even the noblest social goals or visions can become obsessive and oppressive. Human beings need space for an individuality that is not colonized by the demands of consumer culture, the workplace, schools, or the neighbors. The institutions of our consumer society—from our workplaces to our schools and our urban and suburban streets and shopping centers—have long since become undemocratic threats to the individuality we prize.

Homework is one further outpost and manifestation of business civilization. Yet the decision by school administrators and boards to impose more homework is not the result of immediate threats or mandates from a small core of elite business leaders. The connections are more subtle, and perhaps more dangerous. Conventional wisdom in the realms of business and education are used to defend and reinforce wisdom in the other. Thus, business leaders routinely suggest that, just as one must do homework to get ahead in school, so also workers must work long and hard to succeed in the competitive economy. Schools cite the demands and expectations of the workaday world as proof that homework is necessary. When business leaders then chair elite commissions advocating tighter standards and more homework, their wisdom carries weight not primarily because of threats but because their own business practices reflect the standards, and those practices have often been cited by many educators to defend homework requirements.

Nevertheless, even if no formal dictates are in place, the cultural demands that emerge from this process of mutual rhetorical and theoretical support are a threat to our individuality. Just as norms in each area have achieved a kind of self-reinforcing symbiosis, so, too, can changes in one help leverage changes in the other.

Conclusions

One need not be reminded of how much homework is now expected of our children. The recommendation of thirty years ago for one and a half hours a night for high-school students seems to us like a dream. Just as businesses stretch parents' working hours with abandon, schools feel no compunction about adding homework. We read the accounts from the 1930s and can barely imagine a time in which it was O.K. to say that kids needed down time from schoolwork.

I am led to wonder, has medical science proved that kids do not really need fresh air and sunshine? Can the mental-health profession assure us that there is no harm in kids' driving themselves in school all day and then doing hours of homework at night?

Parents and teachers who are beginning to question the value of more and more homework may defy conventional wisdom, but, as we have seen, they have many ancestors who share a vision of a homework-free home. There is a long history of questioning the educational value of homework and of examining the price families and children pay for the practice.

We need to remember that this waxing and waning of opinion on the subject is not mere fashion, however. One way this history can be seen is as corresponding to the pressures of business. Homework has been especially emphasized during periods in which our political and business leaders experienced the need for, and enjoyed the power to be able to reassure both the public and themselves about, certain core values of our business civilization. Their key ideals have included individual initiative, the market, and economic growth. Homework's centrality was effectively challenged and limited during periods in which business leaders were forced to share power with a wider array of interests and concerns.

In the past fifteen years, business leaders and their values once again have come to dominate not only public policy but also much of public discourse. Why business civilization triumphed is a story whose full complexity is beyond the scope of this book.[35] The growing power of the large corporation is surely part of the story. In addition, some who resisted it bought into overly romantic notions about small communities or had a naive or dangerous faith that central government could solve all social problems.

But it is important to realize that throughout our history a variety of divergent groups, including social reformers, some immigrant communities, and many Native Americans, have challenged not only the power of the corporation but also the centrality of economic growth and a life of work without end. Our culture and our politics have benefited from the resistance they offered. The lesson is clear. The best and most enduring communities provide as wide a space as possible for the emergence of alternative perspectives and lifestyles. These are valuable not only to their adherents. The vitality they represent can also become an important social and cultural resource. The social and natural world may well be too protean and unpredictable to be confined or expressed fully by even the best and longest-lived set of core values. And as much as human beings need order, a part of them may also periodically crave or thrive from exposure to a world of whimsical thought, eccentric behaviors, and realms of pure play.

Those who value opportunities for an expanding pluralism and individuality have long regarded democratic politics as a crucial and permanent feature of the good society. Every society needs clear personal norms and social values. Democracy is the best way to achieve values that can be widely supported. But in a fluid world, even the best sets of values and institutions may eventually entail intolerable intrusions or present unforeseen problems. Democracy can and should also provide the opportunity to address these intrusions and limits posed by even the noblest values. But for democracy to serve either function well, citizens need the cultural opening and the economic and political resources to be able to participate in continuing efforts to curb the worst abuses of public and private power.

Unfortunately, however, the great Catch-22 of business civilization lies in its erosion of the very tools needed to curb it. Not only does it foster inequality of economic–and thus political–resources. It deprives citizens of the time needed to engage in political efforts to redress its growing incursions into our lives. The emerging fight over homework is one important effort not only to improve family life but also to free up an important political resource.

Hard work surely enhanced the quality of American life, but so did a politics of time. Our parents lived more satisfy-

ing lives than their ancestors because progressives enacted
tax and wage legislation and labor-law standards that both
place limit on economic inequalities and encouraged reductions of adults' working hours. Experiences from workplaces
and schools each reinforced the other. Progressive educators
argued that students should have more free time, just as
adult workers should. In the process, parents gained more
free time to spend with their children. Workplaces became
more, not less, productive.

The past quarter century has seen erosion of many of
these gains in the quality of life both for children and for
working- and middle-class parents. Business opposition to
reductions in working hours and re-emphasis on homework
are a large part of the explanation. Yet there is a sense in
which labor and progressive activists must bear some of the
blame, as well.

Progressives in the labor and social-justice movements, as
well as progressive educators, had counted on federal and
state policies to ensure in perpetuity freedoms that may be
sustainable only through a commitment to democratization
not only of schools but also of corporations. During the
1960s, many radical and counterculture communities held
a naively individualistic notion of freedom. They assumed
that schools could simply make changes on their own to
ensure individual space and autonomy for the child and that
workplaces would automatically accommodate themselves.

On a more fundamental level, some of the more radical
counterculture groups assumed the possibility of a world in
which everyone could and would do his or her own thing, a
kind of total laissez faire in the realm of culture. In a sense,
they became the ultimate mirror image of the strident and
all-encompassing moralism of the work ethic. They denied

or neglected the role that democratic politics must play in negotiating and periodically adjusting the demands of schools and workplaces to the need for individual space and autonomy. The free-time and cultural opportunities students and workers can enjoy depend on successful and cooperative completion of work and educational tasks.

Rather than moving toward a constructive political engagement over such issues as the kind and amount of work appropriate in our schools and workplaces, the talk of free schools and child-centered learning of the 1960s today has given way to relentless emphasis on standards. The 1920s' talk of a future with twenty-hour work weeks has been replaced by the mantra of competitiveness and the global economy. Yet there are good reasons to suspect that all the work and homework in the world will never make us successful, competitive, or fulfilled in today's global economy.

3

Educating Global Citizens
or Global Workers?

MY FATHER went to medical school during the Depression on $4,000 in gold that his grandfather, who distrusted all banks, had stashed under a bed many years before. During my childhood, I was constantly admonished that assets in any form, even cash, were only paper. The only way to avoid poverty was to "study hard." Long after the New Deal, my father still believed that "you can lose all your savings in stock markets and banks. The one thing you can't lose is your education. As long as you are educated, you can always make it somehow." He believed that homework was the key to success in school and that success in school would keep us out of poverty.

Etched as these words are in my memory, I doubt they make sound public policy.

The United States has a long history of regarding school reform as the key to broader social change. The child is parent of the adult. If the United States, as conventional theories of American exceptionalism hold, has often lacked any strong anti-capitalist reform tradition, school reform has been a big theme.

Nevertheless, earlier ventures in school reform promised far more than they could deliver. Sending young adults into communities and workplaces not ready for their intellect or idealism often does not lead to changes in those institutions. It can just as easily elicit a growing chorus of elite demands that schools heal themselves and learn some "real-world" lessons.

The current emphasis on school failures and school reform is an implicit recognition that all is not well in this "booming" economy. However conservative the current cast in Washington may be, many business and political leaders know that discontent lurks below the surface. They recognize that events such as the December 1999 mass demonstrations in Seattle against the World Trade Organization and corporate-oriented global trade agreements, as well as the periodic outbursts against the International Monetary Fund and corporate globalization, may not be aberrations. Whether sincerely or as the only politically and economically palatable strategy, they now invoke educational reform as the way to ease the transition to a new global economy. Nevertheless, their demands and hopes regarding education are unlikely to be realized. Worse still, much of the education reform they promote may in fact make the lives of many poor and working-class citizens even more burdensome. Unless workers and governments make major changes in our corporate practices, a renewed emphasis on homework and even keeping kids successfully in school all the way through college or a vocational-educational program will still leave growing pockets of poverty and inequality in this society.

On an individual level, of course, it is hard to quarrel with my father's advice. Citizens with the most formal education occupy the upper reaches of law, medicine, engineering, computer science, and business. Even in the face of general declines in working-class incomes, the top fifth of the income pyramid—primarily our lawyers, doctors, engineers, MBAs, and so on—have seen dramatic increases in real income over the past two decades. Robert Reich's symbolic analysts have done quite well.

Observing the success of middle-class professionals leads many policy analysts to make a logical leap. Because success in law, engineering, medicine, and accounting generally is not possible without doing well in school, and because most students with good grades in school study hard, then if everyone studied harder and became more successful in school, more young adults would be able to move into technical and professional positions. Many conservative politicians and business leaders embrace a traditional corollary of this notion. Schools need to be held to stricter standards, students evaluated by those standards, and homework emphasized as an essential key to meeting those standards.

Liberals are more inclined to include equitable and adequate school funding in this recipe, but they also often endorse stricter standards and more homework. The conventional wisdom among both liberals and conservatives then adds the ancillary hypothesis that computerization is opening even more opportunities for the skilled while making life more difficult for those lacking in skills.

As plausible as these claims may seem, every term in this logical sequence may be either totally wrong or seriously flawed. Nevertheless, without a broad political coalition to challenge the entire narrative and build support for related reforms, the homework-intensification movement is likely to grow. Work and homework are part of a broad cultural matrix in U.S. society, and the work ethic is implicated in the formation and evolution of our class structure.

How does the narrative of homework, school success, and progress at work play out in this world? We have already seen that homework at best makes a marginal contribution to academic competence and that it does not explain the success of some highly regarded foreign school systems.

When we move on to the next elements of the equation, a logic utterly blind to the realities of class and economic power continues to prevail. The classical defense of education as a job-creation and job-enhancement strategy has had two elements. The first is the claim that in an increasingly globalized economy, the world will see a division of labor. If the United States wants to be the nation in which corporations locate the challenging and well-paying jobs, policy must ensure the education of our children. The second argument is that technological change itself will open more opportunities for the educated and shrink those for children with fewer educational resources. Let us consider each of these contentions.

Conventional textbooks tell us that breaking down tariff barriers among nations allows each nation to specialize in what it does best. Economies of scale will then lead to rapid advances in wealth for all nations and classes. This is called the neoclassical theory of comparative advantage. This familiar Economics 101 model, however, was constructed in an era before businesses themselves were able or likely to move across borders. Nations exchanged goods and services, but businesses generally stayed put.

Free trade's immediate effect today is to extend to corporations a freedom it denies workers. Free trade is in fact a bit of a misnomer, for it does not simply eliminate government. Both national and supranational authorities play a role in establishing the framework for this trade. Businesses enjoy the right of instant mobility for physical plant and ironclad protections for their "intellectual property" while workers and their rights are non-transferable. Currencies are also even more instantly tradable, so that the very foundations of commerce are subject to speculative forays.

The new trade agreements commence a "race to the bottom." Governments and workers are often forced to cede bargaining power and rights within the workplace to match the lowest national standards. The economist Richard DuBoff, summarizing several studies of the effects of corporate trade treaties, comments: "The mere threat by multinational managers to relocate production abroad may be sufficient to wring wage concessions from their workers, who will nonetheless remain vulnerable to escalated threats in the future."[1]

When the North American Free Trade Agreements (NAFTA) were being negotiated, U.S. Labor Secretary Robert B. Reich argued that lowering all trade barriers between Mexico and the United States could only help our workers, because the Mexicans' tariffs on our goods were higher than our tariffs on their goods. What this argument neglected to point out was that businesses would be reluctant to relocate to Mexico until international trade agreements included protection of corporate rights in the event of expropriation of assets and placed limits on the profits that would be subject to Mexican government taxation. NAFTA does all those things for corporations but is essentially silent with regard to labor rights.

Reich and others also argued that U.S. labor did not have to worry about free trade because only the low-skilled, low-paying jobs would migrate, while the U.S. high-tech industry would enjoy increased markets in Mexico. Yet whole clusters of jobs, including those in both high and low tech, have migrated not because Mexicans are better educated but because comparably skilled Mexicans can be paid considerably less.

The economist Harley Shaiken has shown that modern computer technology allows multinationals to locate even their most sophisticated technology in branch plants all over the globe. Management systems are themselves portable. Shaiken's research on the auto industry shows that Ford can locate a plant in a Mexican *maquiladora*. Workers in that plant may achieve 85 percent of the productivity of their River Rouge counterparts but will receive less than 10 percent of their wages.[2]

The jobs that can be relocated today go beyond even the relatively high-skilled and high-paying industrial jobs. Lester Thurow points out that, despite its well-publicized economic failures, the communist societies did succeed at one thing: They were extraordinarily successful in educating scientists and technicians.[3] With the availability of modern communication techniques, U.S.-based firms today can hire Polish architects and chemists for a small fraction of the salary they once paid to their U.S.-trained counterparts. Even some segments of the professional middle class are not immune to globalism's pressures.

Classical economists who defend world free trade argue that workers always get what they are worth. They are paid in proportion to their productivity. Business economists, however, are able to make this argument only because they assume that unregulated market economies produce automatic full employment. In a full-employment economy, a worker can demand pay levels commensurate with his or her real productivity.

History does not justify the contention that unregulated corporate markets guarantee full employment. Pure free-market societies often lead to great disparities in wealth, as some corporations are fantastically successful while other competitors languish. The very concept of the corporation, with its notions of limited liability and its ability to issue patents and copyrights, have given major corporations extensive economic and political power. Market control often gives corporations both the ability and the incentive to reduce production and drive up prices. Profits grow relative to wages—at least, in the short run. Sluggish wages do translate into lower costs and higher short-term profits and savings for owners. High profits can in turn fuel investment booms, as happened in the United States in the late 1990s. Nevertheless, such booms often lay the foundations of their own demise. Capacity in the popular and widely touted sectors, as was the case with telecommunications in the 1990s, expands rapidly. Yet with wages low and consumer debt growing, markets become saturated. The huge capacity overhangs eventually lead to receding profits, rapid declines in investment, and spreading economic stagnation. The tendency of profits to outstrip wages and to bring about periodic bouts of unemployment to a degree has been muted and counteracted in advanced Western democracies, but only where unions had some freedom to organize and where social policy addressed income disparities. Those freedoms have been increasingly challenged even in industrialized democracies in the past decade.

The situation is worse for the so-called emerging market societies. Mexico is an extremely inegalitarian society in which workers have gained virtually no protection. It has practically never enjoyed a full-employment climate. Whatever one thinks of these extremes from a moral point of view, economically they translate into workers who do not take home enough money to buy the goods modern factories produce. High rates of unemployment in turn keep wages low and put downward pressure on U.S. wages, reduce employment, and undermine unions and other domestic forms of worker protection, such as minimum-wage laws and worker-safety standards.

In addition, U.S. jobs have been lost or wages reduced because of competition with more advanced foreign firms in which workers are well paid but even more productive and innovative. Corporate America, obsessed with short-term profits, fails to use the full talents of its employees. One example is illustrative of broad trends. In the early 1980s, the U.S. auto industry promised it would surpass the Japanese. Japanese manufacturers had pioneered the development of computerized technology that alerts workers when breakdown is imminent.

Japanese businesses are oriented toward tradition and hierarchy, but they differ in important respects from U.S. firms. For example, although Japanese companies lack unions, their pay differentials between management and production workers are far smaller than those in U.S. firms. And although workers have no overall voice in company policy, their production-line skills and talents are seen as a key asset. Japanese firms had made even front-line workers broadly skilled monitors of entire production processes.

General Motors thought it could match Japan by introducing similar technology. But when General Motors introduced its own "smart robots," it omitted one detail: It neglected to teach its workers how to use the robots. The plant soon became one of the least productive in America.[4]

Japan, of course, has struggled economically in recent years. Unemployment has increased, in part because a culture so heavily oriented toward savings and work has been unable to sustain sufficient levels of domestic demand to keep its productive factories fully employed. In addition, its emphasis on skills training of its workers, while laudable, can be carried so far as to discourage broader forms of creativity and even the willingness to challenge basic institutional failings. Nevertheless, Japan still enjoys a balance-of-trade surplus with the United States, not merely because of its own protectionist policies but also because its auto industry continues to be more productive than that in the United States, which still make insufficient use of current workers' skills.

In the context of job flight and related attacks on unions and the social safety net, working-class wages in the United States have essentially stagnated or fallen throughout much of the last two decades. Most families have been forced to rely on two breadwinners to stay afloat. U.S. corporations in turn have responded to the competitive pressures their own global agenda creates by relentlessly reducing labor costs. Their key strategy involves making its core employees work ever longer hours while reducing the rest of its workforce to contingent status.

Many blue- and white-collar workers are now working the longest hours of their lives.

Neither past experience nor the most recent labor-market projections sustain the view that education in our increasingly technological society is the key to greater equity in income. The U.S. Bureau of Labor Statistics predicts that, of the 51 million new jobs created by 2006, 22 million will be in the lowest-skilled category, requiring only short-term on-the-job training.[5] Those service-sector and new-economy jobs are far from what they are written up to be. The heaviest job creation will be for such positions as cashiers, food-counter workers, and security guards. The number of these positions will far exceed that for systems analysts, computer engineers, mathematicians, and database administrators combined.

It is clear that the U.S. economy is already turning out more college graduates than any foreseeable vacancies in these professional fields, a point Susan Ohanian powerfully reinforces:

> The claim is that improved educational standards will lead to a high-skill, high-wage economy. Tell that to the twelve percent of new doctorates in physics who received no job offers. Tell that to the Domino's pizza delivery drivers in the Washington, DC area who have BA degrees. In *Bright College Years* ... Anne Matthews reports that one third of the drivers have such qualifications. She also reports on a warehouse supervisor job ad for the Gap: 'Bachelor's Degree required, and the ability to lift fifty pounds.' ... Corporate thugs have given us a job market where Manpower Inc., the nation-wide temporary employment agency, has surpassed General Motors as the number-one employer.[6]

Ohanian's examples inadvertently illustrate the limits of education as a strategy to alleviate poverty. For many workers, computers have been a double-edged sword. Programming positions are created, but the computer itself makes many skills obsolete. Formerly, cashiers had to be proficient with numbers. Scanning devices have largely eliminated this need. And for all the talk about jobs with computers, most labor economists foresee more job growth among security guards and home health aids.

Even symbolic analysts may be less secure than they imagine. Not only have current trade treaties opened possible competition with elites in well-educated communist nations, but some "less-developed" nations have done an excellent job in educating their elites. Under current trade agreements, "outsourcing" a range of technical and scientific tasks is becoming increasingly appealing to corporations. In a recent investment advisory, Merrill Lynch gushed: "Globalization has morphed beyond making products in low cost areas (a strategy that some other companies are only now implementing) to ... becoming a source of the new core of GE, its intellectual capital. Many engineering and accounting functions are now based in India, with engineering costs dropping ten percent a year."[7]

Jobs have been lost in communities in which U.S. corporations have moved the work to Mexican branch plants or competition with the best foreign plants has simply eroded market share. Some of these jobs have been replaced by service-sector work, but many communities in the old industrial heartland are still worse off than a generation ago. These changes in turn make a mockery of our notions of equality of opportunity. It is not just that jobs are not available to everyone who wants them. In a society in which educational opportunity depends on public schools and those schools are financed primarily by local property taxes, great economic inequality translates into limited educational opportunities. Where jobs are scarce, property values are low, and schools are poor. Because housing in this country traditionally has been segregated not only by racial and ethnic factors but also by income, declines in working-class incomes have differential effects on particular communities.

The "savage inequalities" Jonathan Kozol describes are rooted in the uneven development of our economy, with some regions that have depended on traditional manufacturing employment suffering immensely in recent years.[8] Further-more, growing inequalities and the tendency to seek private escapes from social problems diminishes the will to fund public education at all. As better-off parents either leave declining urban areas or send their children to private schools, the will and ability to fund the inner-city public schools left behind diminishes. As these schools become more disadvantaged, the views of too many citizens about public education are confirmed.

When I think about the despair of the unemployed and the downsized, the vast inequalities in education, and the bull-ishness of Merrill Lynch as General Electric outsources our lives, I am inclined to reverse my father's advice. Most young Americans will not enjoy jobs with adequate salaries and benefits–let alone the opportunity to deploy skills and cre-ativity on the job–unless some of us are willing to take bold action. We need to study less and raise a little more hell. Monitoring our kids' long hours over homework is a zero-sum strategy that will work for fewer and fewer Americans. And paradoxically, emphasizing individual homework as the key to economic security helps reinforce the notion that individuals are at fault for their own poverty and keeps them from having the time or the inclination to participate in polit-ical action that might alleviate their poverty.

Our political leaders do periodically rediscover poverty when elections approach, but the United States is a difficult nation in which to be poor. Puritan New Englanders took hard work and wealth as signs of God's favor. By the nine-teenth century, our culture was dominated by the Horatio Alger mystique of rags to riches. Work hard enough and luck, along with the right young woman, would come your way. The converse of these celebratory ideals lay in the widespread conviction that the poor deserved their fate. That fate reflected a lack of moral centering, often reflected in lazy habits or undue indulgence in drink or other forms of forbidden pleasure. Conservatives were willing to leave the poor to their fate. Corporate and liberal philanthropy offered occasional alms–accompanied by intrusive moral guidance.

For many middle- and working-class Americans, this moral economy provided some solace, albeit often painful, for their hard work and tenuous hold on the American dream. If their days were long and their rewards often sparse, at least they knew work and reward set them off from the shiftless poor. Only during the Great Depression, when poverty gripped wide segments of the middle and working classes, were these easy moral certainties widely challenged.

Such a moral economy may seem like a quaint memory, but it remains alive today in more secular garb. Familiar stereotypes about the poor continue to shape the debate. Many still believe that hunger in a growing economy is proof that the poor are to blame.

But if hunger is a consequence of character flaws, one must wonder why its incidence fluctuates so severely over time and across regions. In 1998 and 1999, political leaders celebrated the shrinkage of the welfare rolls and the entry of many recipients into the regular job market. Though there are good reasons to value diminishing dependence on a paternalistic welfare state, the corporate job market merits as much scrutiny as the welfare system. The majority of the poor are working poor.

National studies conducted by Rutgers University's Center for Workforce Development indicate that only 24 percent of the working poor wanted to work less, compared with 58 percent of other workers from earlier Rutgers studies.

Conversely, 24 percent of the working poor said they wanted to work more, compared with 12 percent of other workers.

The Rutgers study also found that 81 percent of the working poor wanted to enroll in education or training programs, but only 18 percent work for employers who give financial help for off-site job training or education (compared with 36 percent of higher-income workers). Only 27 percent received government aid for that purpose.[9]

Corporate unwillingness to fund job training is not surprising in a corporate culture that emphasizes short-term profits and often fails to make the best use of the existing talents of workers at all levels. The stagnation in workers' pay that has characterized all but the last eighteen months even of the 1990s "boom" accounts for much of the hunger among low-income workers. It also helps reinforce many of the stereotypes and resentments held by those just above them in the corporate pyramid.

The American dream of a stable and secure family life has become elusive, at best. In the context of a corporate culture that seems resistant to change and a political process that is virtually moribund, traditional notions about the poor deserving their fate and being unworthy of aid help some marginalized working- and middle-class citizens sustain a sense of their own worth. Both poor and working-class families often hope to enhance self-esteem, and perhaps attract more corporate help, by stressing their willingness to push their children hard on homework to get ahead.

These trends have important political consequences. If a reform coalition is to be both effective and politically viable, it must be responsive to disparate interests and concerns. Without economic reforms, most Americans are likely to suffer stagnant or declining incomes; alternating bouts of unemployment and multiple long-hour jobs; and a tenuous quality of neighborhood life. Fear and desperation may accompany these conditions. These can often intensify tendencies toward self-blame or hatred of those who are different, especially in a culture that regards hard work and success by one's own bootstraps as American as apple pie. Even those who often stand outside the cultural mainstream will be affected. These cultural "outsiders" often depend to some degree on part-time work within the established business system. Few of us are either completely inside or outside the system, and its travails have serious implications for most of us.

But by the same token, the traditional liberal and working-class concerns about wages and job conditions are unlikely to attract the kind of alliances needed to achieve economic justice within the workplace unless a reform package includes a more generous attitude toward activities in other spheres of life. Blue- and white-collar workers are going to need the support not only of many excluded welfare recipients, but also of those for whom home schooling or subsistence farming or, less radically, the relative self-sufficiency of the family garden, or the open-access forest, or the underground economy are not only survival strategies but part of the good life.

I will offer some hypotheses for future political discussion. They are not totally original; nor have they been, or can they be, fully proved. Nevertheless, there is at least as much evidence for them as for their more conventional counters.

1. Service-sector jobs offer less compensation than manufacturing jobs not because the work is inherently less challenging but because much of this sector is female,

disproportionately staffed by racial and ethnic minorities, and not unionized. Much of the service sector's work involves caring for or listening to others, skills our male and productivist society often devalues. The recent success of primarily female home–health-care workers in California in unionizing for better pay and working conditions may herald a significant change. Direct organization not only by union professionals but also by rank-and-file members promises the most good. Unions that are themselves willing to question past racism and sexism in their organizing and internal politics are most likely to achieve success.

2. For many service-sector jobs to become remunerative, more than labor organization will be needed. Minimum-wage campaigns, already under way in states and communities, have played a vital role in raising the incomes of service-sector workers. Many of these workers are poor not because of any personal failings but because their wages have failed to keep pace with increases in their productivity. These lags in turn are a consequence of attacks on unions and a steady decline in the real value of the minimum wage over the past two decades. Wage standards and the broader working conditions enjoyed by these workers play a major role not only in quality of life but also in educational gains. When businesses must pay a just wage to their workers, they are more inclined to treat these workers as real assets and to both train and respect them. In such a context parents can provide better learning environments for their children and foster examples that build the educational aspirations of them.

Fortunately, a series of ongoing campaigns in many states and cities have attempted to address the plight of underpaid workers. The higher minimum wages achieved, contrary to many conservative attacks, have not cost jobs or injured businesses. These campaigns have taught an important lesson. Grass-roots activism has been the key component here. Politicians from Bill Clinton on down have followed rather than led. Only when it has become clear that grass-roots initiatives were going to demand these standards, or even enact them through local and state referenda, have national political leaders begun to embrace the concept. And even then, proposed federal standards continue to lag behind many local efforts.

3. The experience within many localities and workplaces shows that service-sector jobs need not be low-skill. A progressive corporate minority has attempted to fashion "high-performance" workplaces. Even front-line workers are given some voice in designing the service or product, establishing corporate goals, and fashioning job ladders and training programs. Such businesses have an impressive track record. But these changes are most likely and most effective where workers have organized an independent voice to demand them.

4. The kind of education that is going to yield good jobs is not of the rote, keep your nose to the grindstone and learn a few simple truths sort. It must be education that engages the interests of children and relates to their experiences in communities and workplaces. This does not mean education that is merely aimed to get them a job. It should make the workplace and community experiences of students and their parents a subject of open debate. It would explore the subject of differing models of workplace and community life and invite critical commentary from a variety of perspectives. Good jobs demand well-educated

students, but most will not get these jobs unless there are changes on the demand side, by which I mean the development of a corporate culture and corporate practices that genuinely value their workers as full and equal partners in the enterprise. Such a corporate culture is in turn more likely when new workers have become aware of a broader range of possibilities than our high-school economics and business courses provide.

5. Finally, even the loss of good manufacturing and professional jobs should not be regarded as inevitable. Physicists in India and auto manufacturers in Mexico are as worthy of good jobs as their counterparts in Berkeley or Detroit. Nevertheless, as long as current trade practices prevail, everyone will be whipsawed until wages are near subsistence level everywhere. Only corporate owners will profit. Fortunately, the protests against international trade agreements that have occurred in recent years in such places as Seattle, Washington, D.C., and Davos, Switzerland, suggest that international grass-roots coalitions of workers and environmentalists may force a new charter on multinational corporations. If wage standards, labor rights, and environmental protection are taken as seriously as copyrights and profit repatriation, engineers and blue-collar workers may prosper worldwide.

Imposing wage and environmental standards in trade treaties need not be a protectionist step that disproportionately burdens emerging economies. Standards that emphasize the rights of all workers to organize and openness of and access to manufacturing sites benefit all workers and citizens and facilitate processes of international cooperation among nongovernmental organizations. Education reform, both in the content of formal education and in the stance adopted toward various extracurricular activities and forms of learning, can aid in the development of both citizens who are open to new experiences and patterns of collective negotiation across current national, racial, and cultural boundaries.

More broadly, what role does homework reform play in the total process of fostering economic change? Its role is not only to alleviate time pressures on working- and middle-class families but also to create a cultural space in which constructive dialogue can occur. It has become commonplace to talk about the suspicions among environmentalists, counterculture types, and a range of cultural conservatives both in rural areas and among some urban labor groups. But this has an educational analogue. Some liberal educators who do care about class issues also distrust or devalue what goes on in the homes of many formally uneducated citizens. Nevertheless, most poor and working-class citizens do have agendas for their children. For some, this can be more homework in the hope of exiting the situation in which they live. For others, the agenda includes primarily religious instruction, survival skills and other mechanical talents, outdoor education, swimming and cycling, or the sharing of hobbies and family traditions. Homework closes off many of these agendas. It can lead to angry confrontations between parents and children and neverending efforts to keep the kid on target and to blame him or her when failure ensues. For other parents, it leads to resentment of the schools. For many on both sides of the divide, time pressures intensify the rigidity of one's commitment to his or her concept of family values and eagerness to impose those on others.

For most parents, a traditional liberal reform package—which might include more equitable school funding, an emphasis on union rights, and better wages—is unlikely to tap anywhere near the full range of their resentments. That liberal package is unresponsive to a central concern of their lives: the space and activity they have already carved out or would carve out in their neighborhoods and extended families.

Just as basically, homework is work and must be understood in the context of our work-centered culture. Our children do not come home to Beaver Cleaver's family. As the Economic Policy Institute reported in January 2002:

> In 1998 the typical middle-income, married-couple family worked six more weeks a year than did a similar family in 1989.... Workers are also clocking more overtime hours. Almost one-third of the workforce regularly works more than the standard 40-hour week; one-fifth work more than 50 hours. Hourly manufacturing workers, the only group tracked by government statisticians, are putting in 25% more overtime than they were a decade ago. In virtually every industry within the bellwether manufacturing sector, overtime had reached a record by the end of the 1990s. The growth in overtime work, while helping to drive the healthy growth in output in the U.S., has unhealthy social costs. It is taking its toll not only on workers, but on their families, communities, and, ultimately in many cases, patients, customers, and employers. Families burdened by longer work hours are more likely to find it difficult to balance the conflicting demands of work and family. More hours spent at work mean less time with the family, less time to help a child with homework, less time for play, less time for housework, and less time for sleep.[10]

Even within the two-parent family, *both* parents come home overworked from their jobs and must help children with the work of the school in their own house. This dynamic can point in at least two ways. Some parents are too exhausted and embittered to participate, and homework alienates not merely because it distracts from other agendas but because it is simply more work. For other parents, the dream persists that, if their children can only work hard enough, they might escape the worst aspects of their jobs. They push their children and try to lend what support they can. There is logic to this. A few do escape—at least, from the grind of the assembly line to the safer and more remunerative tedium of law-firm associate or hospital resident.

Unfortunately, such escapes, though the stuff of legend, happen all too rarely, and the rewards of even the good life today seem increasingly hollow. If American conservatism has an Achilles' heel, it is the extremes of wealth and poverty that have emerged in the past two decades. Never an egalitarian lot, conservatives once promised that the magic of the market would make most of us at least comfortably middle class. Government was perceived as the source of monopoly power and extreme inequality. If noxious tax and regulatory policies were curbed, the vigor and skills of everyone would get full play.

A two-decade experiment in corporate economics has yielded a shrinking and more vulnerable middle class. Nevertheless, its defenders remain unrepentant. Their prevailing metaphors have changed, however. Instead of images of middle-class solidity, such as the small-business person, the craftsperson, or the young professional, we have megabucks writ large. Even if life is inherently unfair, with some big winners and losers, everyone has an even chance to win the great lottery of life.

Yet academic and journalistic work increasingly refutes this robust faith in social mobility as the answer to poverty.

The British journalist Will Hutton recently summarized some of the best work on this topic:

> Conservatives try to excuse this inequality by arguing that American income and social mobility is uniquely high, as befits an exceptional civilization. It is not; indeed it compares badly with the Europe about whom American conservatives are so patronizing. Lawrence Mishel, Jared Bernstein and John Schmitt, the three authors of *The State of Working America* (described by [London's] *Financial Times* as the most comprehensive independent analysis of the American labor market), compare the mobility of American workers with the four biggest European economies and three Scandinavian economies. They find that the US has the lowest share of workers moving from the bottom fifth of workers into the second fifth, the lowest share moving into the top 60 per cent and the highest share of workers unable to sustain full-time employment. The most exhaustive study by the [Organization for Economic Cooperation and Development] confirms the poor rates of relative upward mobility for very low-paid American workers.[11]

The presence of a few rags-to-riches Horatio Alger types on lists of America's wealthiest families hardly obscures the disproportionate presence of inherited wealth on such lists. A few conservatives may still wish to contend that, more than inheriting money, the children of the rich and famous inherit ability. Yet such rejoinders, implied by Richard Herrenstein and Charles Murray in the notorious *Bell Curve*, run aground on a host of research demonstrating that human abilities are multifaceted and are heavily responsive to lifelong, supportive environments.[12]

Children of the rich start with enormous financial advantages. The creation of elaborate trusts as well as outright evasion of tax laws leaves these children with very large fortunes at the death of their parents. Even routine reinvestment of these funds and a modicum of financial restraint can yield exponential increases in their wealth.

More basically, equality of opportunity means more than equality of legal rights. We surely may take comfort that the United States is not a caste society, where opportunities are legally limited to those from certain backgrounds or races. Nevertheless, opportunity for advancement must be materially as well as legally grounded.

Families must differ in terms of material amenities if we are to foster incentives for individual initiative. Nevertheless, once gaps in family circumstances become extremely wide, some have virtually no chance of success, and others can hardly fail. Equality of opportunity is little more than a legal fiction in modern societies without ongoing access to medical care, public education, and adequate food and housing. Just how great a gap in wealth erodes equality of opportunity and how best to broaden opportunity is a political question in need of constant attention in a democratic society.

We pay for the growing loss of economic opportunity in more ways than merely our hypocritical celebration of a vanquished ideal. The talents of many are neither stimulated nor challenged, at great cost not only to our economy but to the future of our democracy.

Homework is surely one of the much touted resources of the new generation of potential Horatio Algers. For most parents, however, regardless of their children's or their own inner feelings, it is part of an all too common assault on their time. The best way to get back our time is not to work harder to achieve a vanishing dream of mobility. Rather, most are better off demanding both equitable pay and gradual reductions in the working day, gains that were steadily made throughout much of the post–World War II period, when labor had a much stronger voice in our politics.

Business leaders have repeatedly claimed from the 1930s on that reductions in hours would eviscerate American productivity. As I noted in Chapter 2, they also claim that European labor markets lack of flexibility, especially, and that the far more liberal vacations guaranteed Western European workers have been a major source of the sluggishness of these economies. If you read the business press, you may be excused for concluding that Western Europe is in the midst of economic decay and political crisis. Yet this perspective may be a better reflection of the anxieties of the U.S. press and our business and educational elites than of the experience of most Europeans. Social democracy deserves neither contempt nor unqualified praise. A more nuanced interpretation may offer rewards to progressive business and educational leaders on both sides of the Atlantic.

The business consensus is trumpeted ad nauseam: Germany, the Scandinavian nations, and France suffer from "overly regulated" labor markets and high unemployment. The business press routinely suggests that Europe is in a "productivity slump." European nations endure slow growth in output per worker, whereas the United States sees steady growth.

One problem with this analysis is that worker productivity is defined not as output per worker but as output per working hour. The economist Dean Baker reminds us that, in terms of output per working hour, European productivity has continued to increase at the rate of 1 to 2 percent annually over the past six year. He adds: "The growth in output per hour has not always translated into output per worker, since workers have taken a large portion of the gains of higher productivity growth in the form of shorter work weeks. . . . Work weeks of 35–37 hours are standard in the euro zone nations, as is five to six weeks a year of paid vacation."[13] Some European nations now enjoy higher absolute rates of worker productivity than the United States.

Western Europe has suffered from somewhat higher levels of unemployment, but part of that difference is also definitional. In the United States, we count part-time employees seeking full time employment as fully employed, and we exclude so-called discouraged workers from the labor market. If the U.S. definition of unemployment were used, the former West Germany's current unemployment would stand at around 6 percent, not far off the U.S. case.

So this is the future we are to fear? Unemployment is not markedly higher than our own; workers retire earlier and enjoy more time off; and they are often more productive while working.

Yet even in the midst of a stunning U.S. business scandal, our media continue to tell us how inept and morally lax European nations are. Roy Hattersley, a columnist with the British *Guardian* newspaper, poses an interesting thought experiment:

> Let us pretend that, 10 years ago, the Swedish social fund–by which that country's trade unions helped to manage tax-financed investment in socially desirable projects–had been accused of publishing bogus balance sheets. . . . There is no doubt what the reaction would have been. . . . The scandal would have been denounced, not as an aberration but [*sic*] the result of socialism's inherent weakness. We would have been told that nothing better was to be expected from a system which disturbed the equilibrium of the free market.[14]

European social democracies are and always have been far from perfect. Nevertheless, their greatest deficiencies may lie not in their willingness to discipline labor markets but in their failure to extend democracy to the realms of finance and international trade.

Unemployment in Europe, even when measured properly, is too high. Nevertheless, if one tries to establish a correlation between labor-market regulation and levels of unemployment, one finds almost no relationship. Sweden and Italy are both near the top in terms of percentage of unionized workers, tax rates, and other labor restrictions, but they have enjoyed lower unemployment over the past decade than has relatively more lax Spain. Furthermore, by almost any standard levels of labor-protection regulation in Europe were stronger during the first quarter century after World War II, a period in which European unemployment was generally quite low and rates of growth were robust.

The diverging approaches the European Central Bank and the U.S. Federal Reserve have taken in recent years bears more scrutiny from the U.S. media. In spite of relatively high European unemployment and very low rates of inflation, the European Central Bank has set a short-term interest rate of 3.25 percent, whereas our Federal Reserve has set a rate of 1.25 percent. In addition, the European Union now imposes tight fiscal constraints on its member nations. The size of any member's budget deficit is constrained with the threat that nations going too far into the red will be forced to pay a tax to the European Union.

If Western Europe has more democratic labor markets, it also has fiscal and monetary policies that are a banker's dream. Western Europe is caught in a standoff between central bankers obsessed with controlling inflation and traditional labor and social-democratic concerns about the quality of working-class life. Social democrats are to be blamed not for persevering in efforts to preserve the quality of working-class life but for their hands-off attitudes toward their own central bankers and the broader terms of European union. Unfortunately, this is a story our corporate media do not want to hear.

Fortunately, workplace hours, lack of vacations, and forced overtime are playing a growing role in our politics. Increasing numbers of citizens not only indicate to pollsters that they are concerned about the number of hours they are forced to work; they are active within their unions and other employee associations. In addition, many workers have reached a point at which they are more willing than they have been in many years to consider union membership or other forms of collective worker action as a way to achieve more control over their lives and economic futures. As the labor journalist David Moberg reports:

> Recent polls capture the dramatic shift in opinion. In July [2002] the Gallup Organization found that 38 percent of Americans consider big business to be the "biggest threat to the future of the country," the highest figure in 48 years of polling. In a survey for the AFL-CIO, Peter Hart Research found that 39 percent of Americans have a negative view of corporations (and 30 percent positive), compared with just a year earlier when 42 percent had a positive view (and 25 percent negative)—a massive reversal. At the same time, Hart found that 50 percent of nonunion workers say they would vote yes (with 43 percent voting no) in a union representation election in their workplace, a sharp increase from the 42 percent who said they would vote for a union a year ago. Even the pro-management Employment Law Alliance found that 58 percent of Americans surveyed supported unions organizing more workers, 73 percent favored mandatory representation of workers on corporate boards, and 84 percent wanted pension funds to hold corporations more accountable.[15]

One of the major concerns of workers is the issue of control of time. Nurses in many communities are both joining unions and going on strike to gain reductions in their working hours and combat forced overtime. They argue, with good evidence, that long overtime jeopardizes patient care and disrupts family life. In addition, firefighters in Connecticut recently challenged the constitutionality of mandatory overtime. Although they lost, they made an argument that resonated with many: that forced overtime violates the 13th Amendment ban on slavery. Recent strikes by pilots at such major airlines as United forced the cancellation of hundreds of flights because the pilots were refusing to work overtime. And in a development with the most significance for the so-called new economy, the Verizon telephone strike was settled only after the phone company agreed to cut its overtime demands in half.

With Americans more willing to raise the issue of time both in negotiating with their bosses and in political struggles, homework takes on added significance. On the one hand, many parents want more time so they can assist with homework. They argue, correctly, that if homework is ever to be a valuable practice for many families, they will need more time to assist with–or, at least, monitor–the work. Nevertheless, for many other parents struggles at work lead them to ask exactly the same questions regarding the demands made of their children: Just how much is too much, and is work beyond a certain point really accomplishing all that we think or expect?

In addition, getting back our time may require commensurate reductions in the homeworking day. The school reforms to be discussed in Chapter 4, including elimination of homework for children in the elementary grades, coupled

with substantial improvements in the quality of their schooling and limited independent work for older children in a
safe, secure, setting with suitably trained adults available
for assistance would help free family time for both leisure
and political pursuits.

Unfortunately, in one of the great Catch-22s of modern
life, the only way to get back time on the homework and
workplace fronts is to spend time. None of these reforms is
likely to come through elite or representative strategies. We
are going to have to invest our time in political struggles
with local school boards over the issue of homework policy.

Robert Putnam has famously commented on the ways in
which our society and political culture have become increasingly atomistic. Recreational activities such as bowling, once
pursued through leagues and groups, are now carried on
alone. In addition, Putnam has lamented the loss of social
capital, the rich interest-group structure that historically gave
Americans a more ongoing connection to political issues than
sporadic elections can ever provide.[16]

The Harvard political scientist Theda Skocpol has gone on
to argue that more significant than the collapse of or retreat
from civic groups has been their change:

> In just a third of a century, Americans have dramatically
> changed their style of civic and political association. A civic
> world once centered in locally rooted and nationally active
> membership associations is a relic. Today, Americans volun-
> teer for causes and projects, but only rarely as ongoing mem-
> bers. They send checks to service and advocacy groups run
> by professionals, often funded by foundations or professional
> fundraisers. Prime-time airways echo with debates among
> their spokespersons: the National Abortion Rights Action
> League debates the National Right to Life Committee; the
> Concord Coalition takes on the American Association of

Retired Persons; and the Environmental Defense Fund counters business groups. Entertained or bemused, disengaged viewers watch as polarized advocates debate.[17]

The increasing role of the media and of money in our political life is surely one cause of this phenomenon, but time pressures play a role, as well. Individuals involved in the tasks of work and homework simply have too little opportunity to become active participants in organizations, even when they still belong. The major contribution they can make is money. These organizations in turn almost inevitably come to rely on the judgments and activism of senior staff and the ability of that staff to raise funds. The role of media and money in politics thus becomes both cause and consequence of diminished forms of direct political participation. But this vicious circle can be made to spin in the opposite direction.

School reform can play a central role not only in changing schools but in reshaping political commitments. Many parents still are willing to devote a disproportionate amount of their time to their children and to local politics, especially time spent volunteering in schools, attending school-board meetings, or even working on behalf of local board candidates. A school-reform agenda that includes homework reform as a major component would offer several advantages. It would engage parents who are traditionally divided by contentious social issues. Many socially conservative parents, who often already enjoy a greater degree of political mobilization, would embrace the cause. Middle-class parents, who also enjoy relatively more opportunities and capacity for effective political participation, might also choose to become involved. Finally, in politics success often breeds more interest and engagement, and the struggle to limit homework can be won at the local board level. Even without greatly increased funding for schools, freeing teachers' and parents' time from often useless and counterproductive homework can improve the quality of education.

Success in this area would have the positive spinoff that it would not only free family time; it would free time for other struggles, as well. Action on these other fronts that both demand our time and sap our just rewards will be necessary if school reforms are to be sustainable. Without victory in these other struggles, I fear, many parents will still envisage no other escape for their children but to drive them harder, regardless of what the research shows, even if homework is reduced. And overworked parents who have too little time and energy for homework now will still have too little time for alternative family-centered agendas that are part of childhood growth. Without challenging and limiting our traditional love affair with work, the private corporation, and individual initiative across the board, the old order is likely to reassert itself not only at the school-board level but in many families, as well.

If families in a stagnant and inegalitarian economy may see no other escape besides more homework, political and business elites will also continue to have ample reason to push homework, regardless of its academic pedigree. Homework can always take new forms. Whatever failure the research may suggest for one homework mode, there is, as with Tide, always the new and improved. Furthermore, homework intensification is school reform on the cheap. It costs less than equalizing school funding, both politically and fiscally. And it hardly challenges any vested interest.

A quarter century ago, Samuel Bowles and Herbert Gintis's classic *Schooling in Capitalist America* maintained that our schools were one area in which the battle between labor and capital was carried out. Capitalists, acting through politics, think tanks, and foundations, tried to alter the structure of secondary and post-secondary education in ways that would prepare workers for a class-stratified work process. Tracking was a major part of their emphasis, along with the formation of a multi-tiered school system.

I would argue today that the very stress on homework and the long school day is another, and increasingly problematic, form of this preparation process to accustom the student worker to long working hours. In addition, not only is homework a form of psychological preparation, but both the form and content of homework is designed to send the cardinal message of today's business civilization: This is a competitive world whose purpose lies in endless production. Our ability to multiply material affluence is portrayed as proof of our ability to know and control that world and thus a testimony to our personal rectitude.

The form and content of that message distract us from the ways in which human decisions and cultural values have in fact made that competitive world what it is and the ways in which social choices have turned economic growth into an imperative shaping our lives. They attempt, though unsuccessfully, to still the doubts and resentments many of us harbor regarding what we give up to sustain this business civilization.

Education is important, but not solely for the reasons usually cited. For education to be a genuinely progressive force in American life, it must put some of these issues into play. For this kind of reform to happen, it will require a politics that addresses not only schools but also the many social institutions and practices that constrain them. In short, education will never pay off for most citizens until we devote as much effort to our politics as to our studies. Our politics must take the free time of not only workers but also students and parents as seriously as it regards work. In the long run, our schools, our workplaces, and our families would be the better for it.

As the experience of progressive educators in the 1930s and 1960s demonstrates, education reforms, however defined, cannot fully reverse the patterns of poverty and exploitation that are also rooted in the corporate economy. Indeed, some might argue that progressives inadvertently buy into business leaders' willingness to place blame on schools rather than the economy by participating in the school-reform debate at all.

School reform is, however, topic A in American life, and failure to address it from a progressive perspective will only marginalize those interested in greater economic justice. And even if education reform cannot by itself ease prevalent inequalities, it must be part of the process. Progressives can enter the debate in ways that not only highlight inequalities in contemporary public education but that also point to broader problems in the corporate economy. Issues growing out of homework, exacerbated as they are by state and corporate pressure on schools, teachers, and working parents, are one excellent and thus far too neglected pivot. Teachers interested in smaller classes and better professional training are more likely to gain broad public support by reaching out to other related causes. Support for the kinds of parental needs that also contribute to education, such as adequate wages and training opportunities and more free time for families, are important in themselves and a means of building broader coalitions. The form and content of school reforms can themselves contribute to the construction of these coalitions.

There are at least four guidelines that a school-reform movement attentive to equality should observe. First, reforms should avoid lending rhetorical support to the blame-the-poor mindset. Asserting that students, especially those from poor backgrounds, lag behind their middle-class peers primarily because of a lack of self-control fails to recognize the many forms of discipline many poor children must display on a daily basis. It also fails to acknowledge that the circumstances in which poor children must do their homework ensures further problems—especially in the deficient schools most of these children attend.

Second, progressive educational reform must not rob the poor of their greatest asset: the power to mobilize. Time is the scarcest of modern commodities. The increased time pressure on poor families from both work and homework are a major contributor to our decline in civic participation. Poor parents and their children are more likely to thrive if parents go to school boards and legislatures to lobby for more education funding, a decent minimum wage, and adequate labor standards

Third, any package of school reforms must seek to build bridges between the poor and working and middle class parents. In this context, homework reform must not become or be seen as a middle-class luxury that the privileged middle class imposes on the poor, thereby denying them any chance to escape poverty. Those committed to education reform, including teachers who seek more adequate working conditions and parents of middle-class children who feel oppressed by homework and long hours of their own work, are more likely to garner needed support from poor and minority communities to the extent that those communities feel the reforms have their interests at heart. Middle-class groups seeking alternatives to homework are more likely to receive a sympathetic hearing if they also support economic reforms that expand opportunities for poor and working-class communities.

Fourth, homework reform must not become a license to run roughshod over strategies that some poor and working-class communities may, however shortsightedly, see as their ticket out of poverty. I am not in favor of state or national policy to "ban" homework. Rather, I wish to evoke more widespread local conversations about it and to facilitate options so that more schools can experiment with alternatives to it. How such conversations can become a larger part of school-reform agendas will be discussed in the next chapter.

To some poor parents, homework is likely to seem the only way out as long as their neighborhoods continue to languish and state and federal policy continues the underfunding and underdevelopment of poor inner-city schools. Teachers, inner-city parents, and working- and middle-class parents might be able to unite behind more adequate funding and broader mechanisms for parental choice within public schools. I believe that, with ample resources, many schools across the socioeconomic spectrum would be able to demonstrate the efficacy of alternative approaches to homework. If my argument is correct, and if all parents enjoy equal and adequate public educational resources, educational alternatives to homework intensification will spread far beyond a few privileged or venturesome school districts.

4

Education at the Epicenter

When the *New York Times* published an article in October 2000 on the new homework policy in Piscataway, New Jersey, it evoked a familiar set of responses. One reader wrote to complain, "Despite homework's increasingly onerous reputation, Americans desperately need to keep pace with a competitive, interconnected global community. Discouraging students from opening a book over the weekend hardly seems the most effective way to approach education in the twenty-first century."[1]

The reader joined a nearly two-decade litany of complaints and worries about U.S. schools. At least since *A Nation at Risk,* critics have claimed that U.S. schools are insufficiently rigorous and are responsible for the major failings of the U.S. economy. More recently, Louis Gertner, the CEO of IBM, put the case in language reminiscent of Admiral Rickover: American students "come in last or next to last in virtually every international comparison."[2]

By the presidential campaign of 2000, education had moved to the center of American politics. Its leading role had both short-term and long-term causes. After nearly a decade of economic expansion, many of the constituencies on which a Democratic candidate normally relies had achieved relatively few gains. Not only had working-class incomes barely reached the level of the Reagan-era boom, but poverty rates remained stubbornly high. Whatever Clinton-era welfare reform had done to redress working- and middle-class anger at a government viewed as helping the poorest but indifferent to the working middle, it had not benefited the poorest citizens. In addition, working- and middle-class Americans felt increasingly vulnerable to trade-oriented job losses and had seen continual increases in their working hours.

Unwilling or unable to break decisively with Bill Clinton on the trade and welfare policies he had defended as vice-president, Al Gore nevertheless had to offer something to address popular concerns. More generous funding for schools became a natural for him, and coupling those spending proposals with renewed emphasis on testing helped shore up his reputation as a "New Democrat," who places fiscal prudence and personal and institutional accountability at the center of his politics.

For George W. Bush education also played a pivotal role. Because states have always had a much larger responsibility for public education than the federal government, it allowed him to claim tangible political accomplishments in an area of widespread public concern. In addition, Bush strategists correctly reasoned that Republicans were unlikely to win without reaching beyond the traditional base of social conservatives and business elites. The party needed to show concern for ordinary citizens without alienating its base thereby. Bush, too, endorsed added funding for education and greater reliance on standardized testing to assess the results. Only in a rather tepid endorsement of vouchers and in his eagerness to test teachers as well as schools did he separate himself from his Democratic rival.

Whatever their differences, the mainstream leadership of both parties shares the conviction that inadequacies in the U.S. economy can be explained by the poor performance of our schools. Our major foreign competitors do a better job of educating their children and consequently outperform us in the workplace. They work those children longer and harder and subject them to more rigorous standards.

Yet every aspect of this catechism is open to question. Even if one accepts, as I do not, the notion that a school's performance on standardized tests is an adequate measure of its success, the constant criticism of U.S. performance on such tests in international comparisons is misplaced. As Gerald Bracey points out, the reiteration of national standings on various standardized tests has become a kind of unexamined mantra.[3]

I would add that this mantra serves four questionable purposes. It reinforces an unexamined faith in standardized testing; pushes communities to re-emphasize strict tests and often more homework; and deflects attention from consideration of more equitable and democratic reforms that educators and activists might explore. Finally, it distracts us from growing political and economic problems in these much celebrated competitors and the ways that work and homework are becoming worldwide concerns.

As Bracey points out, reports of the international shame of American education are highly exaggerated. Even if one accepts standardized tests as a good measure of educational excellence, the United States is hardly the laggard it is widely portrayed as. In the first place, the United States' rank in the standings depends on the subject matter being tested and on who is tested. In reading, American students are outstanding:

In the major comparative study of reading, conducted in 1992, American students finished second in a comparison of 31 nations. The only students who did better came from Finland, a small, homogeneous country.... And the Finns, of course, have no immigrant population that needs to be taught Finnish as a second language, which might be a daunting task. The top 10 percent, 5 percent, and 1 percent of American students were the best in the world at both ages tested, 9 and 14. In other words, our best readers outscored the best readers in all other nations that participated in the test, even the Finns.[4]

Yet political and business leaders seldom advertise these test results. As Bracey remarks, "I am convinced that if a study comparing American and Japanese students found the Americans finished ahead, the headlines would read: 'Japanese Students Second; Americans Next to Last.'"[5]

U.S. students did not do as well in math and science, but even here the stated test results are better than the elite presentations of this material would suggest. In the mid-1990s math and science tests, U.S. students

got 53 percent of the items right, while the international average was 55 percent. American fourth graders, on the other hand, finished above average, ranking twelfth of 26 nations. In science, American eighth graders were slightly above average, scoring 58 percent correct compared to an international average of 56 percent. At the fourth-grade level in science, American students finished third among the 26 countries. However, only about 15 percent of American students scored as high on TIMSS [Third International Math and Science Study] math as the average Japanese student, while about 39 percent of American students scored as well as 50 percent of the Japanese students in science. Overall, then, American students are near the top in reading, just below average in math, and just above average in science.[6]

Although these scores surely do not justify apocalyptic rhetoric, Gertner and others would still maintain that math and science are the key to international competitiveness and that finishing in the middle of the pack is not good enough for Americans. Yet even if we accept for the moment the way business elites implicitly slight both the economic and political importance of literature, social studies, and the arts, these results are insufficient to justify the sweeping push for tighter standards and longer homework.

As Bracey points out, all international test results are also heavily influenced by just who takes the test. Singapore, for instance, is regularly a leader in these comparisons. Yet Singapore has in effect loaded the dice in support of its performance in this scholastic Olympics:

> Many poor people cross into Singapore each day from Malaysia, do the low-level service jobs, and return home, sparing Singapore the task of educating their children. Longer-term "guest workers" from the Philippines and Indonesia also leave their families behind. In addition, some Singapore families of means whose children are not doing well in the Singapore educational system send their children to school in Malaysia, while some Malaysian children who score well on tests are admitted to the Singapore schools. The relevant numbers aren't available; these are not the kind of statistics that the dictator of Singapore, Lee Kuan Yew, likes to see made public. But Singapore may well get its high scores by exporting low-achieving students, while importing high-achieving students.[7]

Even in the case of the Japanese, comparing tests can hardly justify sweeping conclusions about the need for tougher standards or more homework. Culture plays an enormous role in educational attainment. As Bracey points out:

> For Asian teenagers, getting into the right high school and then the right college are life-determining events. Kazuo Ishizaka, president of the Japanese Council on Global Education, observes, "Japanese society tends to judge people on

the basis of the schools they attended, rather than their ability and skills." Children in Japan often come home from public school at 3:30 in the afternoon, eat, and go on to a private school or tutor. They attend school on Saturdays, and many go on Sundays as well.[8]

In another practice that is just as damning for proponents of tough tests and homework, Japanese schools widely practice social promotion (whereby students are promoted to the next grade based on their age, regardless of actual academic achievement) through the first six grades of elementary school. Tests play a major role, but only after completion of grade six. An emphasis on social promotion is part of the Japanese sense that social solidarity matters and group discipline is crucial. That these six years are then followed by a draconian test with lifelong consequences should not distract us from the ways these schools hardly reflect U.S. faith in working alone at home. The demands and stress they place on students and families are not easily replicable in our culture and are an increasing concern of Japanese families and political leaders. Nor is such an approach necessary for academic or economic success.

Where their schools clearly are ahead is in teacher training and professional development, curricular emphases, and management of the school day. Leon Botstein, president of Bard College (Annondale-on-Hudson, New York), points out:

> In all the countries that outperform us in math and science ... a higher percentage of teachers has extensive training in the subject matter they teach. Their degrees are not in that amorphous field called education. A 1996 Education Department survey revealed that the majority of American math and science teachers do not have academic degrees in math or science. These teachers are entirely dependent on state-mandated, second-rate textbooks and teaching manuals.[9]

Not surprisingly, math education differs considerably in U.S. schools. Bracey points out that "another TIMSS analysis showed that Japanese teachers were much more apt to give an elaborated explanation of a mathematics concept than American teachers were."[10] He goes on to comment in a related comparison of U.S. and Japanese schools that

> American textbooks are about three times as thick as those of other nations and . . . our teachers try to teach it all, often covering topics only briefly and shallowly. . . . American lessons were devoid of mathematical proofs. About 10 percent of German lessons and more than half of the Japanese lessons contained such proofs. American teachers stated concepts, but did not develop them. Only 22 percent of the lessons in this country contained developed topics, compared to 77 percent in Germany and 83 percent in Japan. Not only did German and Japanese teachers develop topics; they linked them to other topics. When lessons were rated on the interrelatedness of their parts, German lessons scored four times as high as American lessons, Japanese lessons six times as high.[11]

Looking at teaching methods and performance, Bracey and others conclude that "the United States . . . has one of the best-educated and most poorly trained teaching forces in the world: Many more of our teachers have advanced degrees than teachers elsewhere do, but other nations provide more internships and on-the-job training to prepare future teachers and to sustain them as professionals."[12]

As correct as Bracey and Botstein are in pointing to the content deficit for many teachers, teaching will never depend solely on knowledge of content or on one-size-fits-all methods of teaching. As master teachers are often likely to point out, the art of teaching is knowing when a student is best left alone and when that student is ripe to receive your help.

That moment is different for different students. Unfortunately, the push to impose a narrow set of standards by administrative fiat will neither encourage such teaching nor succeed in weeding out those teachers who are utterly tone-deaf to the needs of real children.

Even in time management, Japanese schools can teach some lessons, but not the lessons often drawn by the advocates of long homework and tough standards. In a new book about how U.S. public schools use and misuse time, my former colleague Etta Kralovec conveys the following humorous but illustrative story:

> In a moment that can stand as an ironic summary of the issue of quality of time spent in the classroom, candidate Al Gore, during the 2000 Presidential election, was speaking in an honors level history class in a Maine high school. That night on the national evening news we caught a few minutes of his teaching. In the background, we heard a voice over the loudspeaker requesting that a student come to the front office. I guess we could take comfort in the fact that even for the Vice-President schools do not turn off their loud speakers![13]

Such frequent interruptions in classrooms are hardly unusual. Once again, comparative international data also show that "American classrooms were interrupted about one-third of the time, whereas Japanese classrooms never suffered interruptions." Kralovec provides a good discussion and analysis of the cultural and political factors leading to these interruptions:

> The real issue is whether academic learning time should be foregone for what Deborah Meier calls "the sideshows of education." For many teachers the line in the sand, for instance, is the length of the class period because they know that class time is the least sacred commodity in the school and is

encroached on by sports related events in the form of loud-speaker announcements; by parents in the form of deliveries of forgotten lunches; and by "the system" in the form of roll takers and compliance announcements over the loudspeaker.[14]

Kralovec adds:

Parents have a strong desire to be involved in the school in significant ways, yet most of us would be surprised to know how much instructional time is turned over to activities that are only tangentially related to academic learning. For example, full afternoons can be lost because parents hold birthday parties for their children at school. Fund-raising activities in the upper grades can consume energy and time as students are asked to raise the money needed for end-of-the year trips.[15]

There is increasing attention to the problem of lost time in classes, but unfortunately the form that much of that discussion has taken once again reflects the centrality of the work ethic. Rather than seek to keep the focus of allotted classroom time on core academic subjects, many boards and administrators now wish to cut or reduce physical education and eliminate recess. Ohanian comments perceptively on an Atlanta principal's war against recess:

A five-year-old in Atlanta commented to a *Times* reporter, "I'd like to sit on the grass and look for lady bugs." But the Atlanta public schools, like a growing number of districts across the country, have eliminated recess from the school day. Who can read this without weeping? The standards mania has brought us to the point of making children too busy for lady-bugs. . . . Treating a kindergartner like a robot–or a Wall Street broker-in-training–cannot come to a good end.[16]

In language very similar to that of the political theorist William Connolly, Kralovec provides a full rationale for Ohanian's complaints:

Educators have known for a while that play and cognitive development are associated. In the nineteen-thirties, Lev Vygotsky, a learning theorist, found that a key component of play is that it gives children an opportunity to act beyond their age:

> "Play creates a zone of proximal development in the child. In play, the child always behaves beyond his actual age, above his daily behavior: in play, it is as though he were a head taller than himself. As in the focus of a magnifying glass, play contains all developmental tendencies in a condensed form and is itself a major source of development."[17]

Physical-education programs have faced the same relentless downsizing attacks, even in the face of a well-documented obesity epidemic among our children. Yet, as Kralovec points out,

> Beyond the physical activity that students engage in during recess, physical education classes provide another opportunity during the school day for students to build the important social, physical and emotional skills associated with sports. In schools, the athletic budget, which covers the after school athletic programs and the budget of physical education classes are two different categories. The physical education program, which all students are required to participate in, captures a much smaller amount of the identifiable sports budget of any school.[18]

Rather than deprive children of the physical and emotional release they need, better use should be made of the time spent in classrooms. The interruptions in classroom activities for various announcements not only take time from teaching but also break everyone's concentration. Nor are they in any sense free time for the children in those classrooms. In an era of diminished resources and continual efforts to impose standards on schools, it is curious that the broad subject of the erosion of school time—and school budgets—by agendas and concerns that are at best peripheral to learning, such as community fund-raising, pep rallies, and big-time interscholastic athletic contests, receive such little attention. In this regard, comparisons with most European and Asian school systems would pose important challenges.

Perhaps the largest disservice performed by the ways in which most of our business and educational leaders do their international comparisons is that they treat U.S. schools as a monolith and obscure the differences among them. Take Illinois as an example. David Berliner, an education professor at Arizona State University, points to an interesting and under-reported story of twenty public-school districts north of Chicago that serve predominantly wealthy suburban children. These schools "gained permission to compete in TIMSS as a separate nation. Statistically, these public school students are on a par with the top scorers internationally in mathematics and science."[19]

Berliner contrasts these public schools with others in southern Illinois, where scores lag considerably behind U.S. and world norms. These children have "been served by dismal schools—an embarrassment to a nation as rich as ours. Yet any good, random sample of U.S. schools for any international assessments includes both kinds of districts, those similar to East St. Louis and those that resemble the North Shore of Chicago. Put them together, and you hide important distinctions between schools in different communities."

No one would argue that American schools, even its better ones, would not benefit from reforms. But before we embrace "reforms" that would impose significant further burdens on children and parents, it behooves us to look at alternatives that can be shown more reliably to produce adequate test results without also entailing many of the negatives that the testing and homework crazes impose. These alternatives are at least as well supported by international comparisons and scholarly literature and are therefore at least as justifiable–unless our only real agenda is to reinforce certain conventional cultural values and stereotypes.

How curious it is that so many U.S. educational and business leaders now seek to embrace tighter standards and longer hours just at a time that even Japan itself is in economic crisis and many of its leading business and education leaders concede that social workaholism is not merely a psychological problem but an economic barrier to innovation and creativity of the culture. Japanese production-line workers may be more facile in using math to readjust existing products, skills they have gained not merely through schools but through business practices that encouraged their use. Nevertheless, many Japanese leaders now worry that these workers have spent so much of their lives in nose-to-the-grindstone work in narrow cognitive tasks that they are unlikely to be broadly creative. In addition, a culture fixated on work and saving can hardly spend the money needed to keep its productive plants fully employed. Even the Japanese Education Ministry now recognizes that the rigid emphasis on long school hours must be re-examined.[20]

Education clearly is one key to a prosperous future for all children, although, as we have seen, without equally broad political and economic reforms, workers everywhere will continue to experience declining fortunes. These political and economic reforms are, however, just the sort that an emphasis on more homework and tougher standards obscures and makes more difficult. Even in the field of education itself, there are ample reasons to suspect that an emphasis on more equal and adequate education is far more defensible. A close look at the Bush agenda reinforces these concerns.

As he promised during his 2000 campaign, President Bush has given priority to education in his proposals to Congress. Reading election returns and polling data, Bush tried to soft-pedal his most radical ambitions and concentrate on areas of broader consensus. Nevertheless, the president and many conservative Republicans will continue to advocate vouchers. And much in the set of reforms that he and many Democrats share, especially an emphasis on standardized testing, may inadvertently give momentum to vouchers. Although Democrats and moderate Republicans won initial battles on the legislative front during Bush's first two years in office, they would do well not only to make the case against vouchers but also to delineate progressive alternatives.

Scholars have debated voucher experiments for more than a decade. Although proponents of vouchers argue that giving children the opportunity to leave failing public schools boosts educational performance, results appear mixed, at best. Martin Carnoy provides a careful summary of the literature in a recent essay.[21] He points to deficiencies in the control groups with whom voucher recipients have been compared. Most studies have failed to draw a random sample of those students from urban public schools whose parents did not apply for vouchers. These parents were presumably more satisfied with their schools. Follow-up tests to measure success of the private schools have been voluntary, and participation has been low. Results may be subject to a self-selection bias. Those children for whom schools have been a positive experience may be more willing than others to take the voluntary evaluations.

Even if one were to concede that children transferring to private schools do accomplish more than equivalent peers in public schools, our policy conclusions should be guarded. These private schools may be doing well not because they are private but because they benefit from smaller class size or more adequate facilities.

Policymakers must consider not only the educational effects on students who leave public schools but the burdens imposed on those who remain within the system. Under Bush's proposal, students would be free to take a federally subsidized voucher and leave schools failing to achieve gains on standardized tests within a three-year period. Schools that commit themselves to this experiment would receive enhanced federal subsidies. Unfortunately, the amount of money being offered is far too small to fix the massive inequities and long-term underfunding of the poorest schools. Judging those schools by one standardized test will even exacerbate their problems. It will discourage creative teaching and drive the best teachers away.

Bush's proposed vouchers themselves, at $1,500, are too parsimonious. That amount will not pay tuition at even a mediocre private school. One thousand five hundred dollars would probably allow some middle- and upper-middle-class students to leave public schools more easily, but less affluent children would be left behind. For the wealthiest parents, the $1,500 would be little more than a gift for an action already taken. For most poor and working-class families, the Bush program would not make it even remotely possible to afford the $5,000 to $10,000 tuition most private schools charge.

Once such voucher programs were put in place, a destructive dynamic would unfold. More wealthy parents, who already wield disproportionate political influence, could no longer be counted on to support the state and local taxes on which vigorous public education has depended. Public schools would deteriorate, and their students might fall further behind.

Progressives ought to fight for more generous and equitable public education. Solid evidence of how can be found not only in the more complete reading of the international comparisons discussed earlier but also in a Rand Corporation study of educational progress in the fifty states. Smaller classes, more emphasis on teacher training, and better and more inclusive early-childhood programs have consistently advanced educational excellence.[22]

The case for better and more accessible programs for early-childhood development is especially strong. A recent study for the Economic Policy Institute by two University of Michigan researchers indicates that the inequalities in opportunities for cognitive development with which children begin school are substantial:

> There are many factors preventing education from serving this role as "the great equalizer." Schools serving low-income students receive fewer resources, face greater difficulties attracting qualified teachers, face many more challenges in addressing student's needs, and receive less support from parents. This inequality of school quality is widely recognized.
>
> But the inequalities facing children before they enter school are less publicized. We should expect schools to increase achievement for all students, regardless of race, income, class, and prior achievement. But it is unreasonable to expect schools to completely eliminate any large pre-existing inequalities soon after children first enter the education system, especially if those schools are under-funded and over-challenged.... Disadvantaged children start kindergarten with significantly lower cognitive skills than their more

advantaged counterparts. These same disadvantaged children are then placed in low-resource schools, magnifying the initial inequality.[23]

The implications of work by the Rand Corporation, international comparisons, and the Economic Policy Institute study all argue for the importance of programs to improve reading readiness and prepare children for entry into school. The Rand studies indicate that targeting such programs to low-income communities would yield academic benefits that more than pay for their costs. Even some conservative economists argue that the United States should spend more on such programs, but today such popular and successful programs as Head Start fail to enroll even a majority of eligible children.[24]

If the president wishes to insist on vouchers, progressives should turn the tables on him. An adequate voucher system should provide equal educational empowerment to all. Every student should have the opportunity to attend a school as well funded as Phillips Exeter Academy. Because vouchers of this magnitude for the entire school-age population would be prohibitively expensive, funding should be concentrated on those who most need it. Robert Reich has suggested a progressive voucher arrangement under which the poorest parents would receive the largest educational voucher, with amounts scaled back as parental income increases.

Public education is at a crossroads. Public education has always been both a product of and support for deepening political democracy. Republicans rightly insist that public accountability must accompany new public funding. Nevertheless, they are wrong in suggesting that accountability can be achieved best through standardized tests and a right of exit to the relatively better off. When such exit risks destroy the schools and hurt students who remain behind, it is irresponsible. Unfortunately, the process of exit from the public schools is likely to be speeded by the growing emphasis on the other current mantra of educational reformers, one shared by many Democrats: standardized testing.

Even the staunchest advocates of public education would hardly argue that it is above reproach. Schools need to be improved, but since when must improvement be equated with the ability of students to score well on one set of narrowly defined tests devised and implemented by an "expert" cadre? When educational reform is hijacked by the standardized-test mania, its only effect is to reinforce the class and racial biases of American education. The movement for standards is part of the widespread concern that teachers are not being held "accountable" for the success of their students. The success of a school—and even the compensation of its teachers—should be determined by how well students answer a set of standardized questions. The use of one or a few standardized tests to assess schools is deemed necessary because absent an "objective" yardstick imposed by an outside authority, the assumption is that schools will slack off. If students are measured using complex and flexible criteria designed in collaboration by parents, children, and educators, all hell presumably will break out.

Yet, as Ohanian has pointed out recently, in many states the tests are kept secret and the authors are themselves not held accountable for the breadth and sophistication of the questions they ask. She cites the example of a Chicago teacher who is being sued for revealing the following question: Economic systems determine which one of the following: 1) which trade should take place, 2) food and language,

3) how much goods are worth, 4) which people should be employed in certain jobs.[25] A quarter century as a teacher of political economy and a journalist leaves me ill prepared to answer such a question.

Even when schools know more about what to expect on tests, the test craze often puts teachers and administrators in a Procrustean bed. The education writer Alfie Kohn points out that one result of the test craze is a destructive form of competition among schools. Schools teach to the standardized test. Test-taking techniques and the probable content of these tests become the instructional core. As Kohn remarks: "The dirty little secret of American education in the late 1990s is that the intellectual life is being squeezed out of classrooms because policy makers who don't know very much about how children learn have decided it's time to get tough."[26] One consequence is that many of the most creative teachers are leaving public education. A second consequence is that schools themselves become more uniform and rigid.

The standards movement imposes a set curriculum on teachers and in effect de-skills teachers. "How else are teachers supposed to feel except helpless in the face of being told to deliver a curriculum that is invented by external authorities?" Ohanian says. "Nationwide we have the lowest rentention rate of teachers in history."[27]

An approach that strives to improve education by emphasizing standardized testing is probably self-defeating even on its own terms. The schools that have done very well on tests, such as those in the Chicago suburbs mentioned earlier, hardly simply teach to the tests. These are schools that have small classes, individualized instruction, and a range of cultural offerings in the arts, theater, and music. They have the best teachers. As Ohanian puts it:

Those schools have been using different yardsticks for generations: Gifted programs, honors and advanced placement classes. There is no better predictor of success in school than the level of schooling attained by one's parents.... So the standards circling the land are based on inheritance, and, in the end, these standards will be used to blame the victim. Standardistos will proclaim: "We gave them equal educational opportunities. It isn't our fault they didn't pass calculus."[28]

Pushing underfunded urban schools to focus curricula on standardized tests will lead to further reductions in already limited offerings and drive better teachers away. As these schools continue to fail, further fuel will be provided for the voucher push.

Perhaps the greatest need our public schools face is one of the oldest, more equitable funding. Public schooling has always failed some children, in part because in practice we have never honored our ideal of equal opportunity. In most states, local economic development, generally quite uneven across the state, determines the level of funding for our public schools. A town's revenue from property-tax collection is then used as the primary source of funds for schools. The secondary source of funds comes from the state through a variety of grants, programs, and a complicated calculation of local need designed to determine what the state's contribution to local funds will be. In part, this system is an attempt to standardize school funding across the state, but in most states such formulas have never fully come close to equalizing funding. Kralovec comments that this situation

has meant that in some states the discrepancy in school spending between high wealth and low wealth districts is enormous. In many states, you can tell the wealth of a town by the percentage of school funds that come from the state–

the higher the percentage of state funds, the lower the local property tax rate.

Schools calculate a "per pupil cost," which refers to the amount of money that the school needs to educate one student. These costs vary widely across the state. In some states, one district might have a $5,600 per pupil cost, while at a school across town, the figure is $9,000.[29]

Federal initiatives could bridge many of the gaps both within and between states, but the federal role in public primary and secondary education remains quite small. Late in the Clinton administration, funds were allocated to hire additional teachers and to initiate the process of fixing dilapidated buildings. Nevertheless, as the economists Barry Bluestone and Bennett Harrison suggest, "the total amount of additional funds pales in comparison to what many educators think is necessary to improve our public schools."[30]

Conservatives are right in suggesting that schools fail for other reasons, as well, but the proper response is not to gut public education but to find ways to make public education more accountable to the public it serves. Public-school parents and children need more, not less, freedom to innovate. Deborah Meier, principal of the Mission School in Harlem, has long been an opponent of vouchers and an advocate of greater choice within the framework of the public-school system.[31] She believes that small groups of parents should have access to the facilities and funds proportional to the number of students they will serve in order to design their own forms of schooling. Such schools would not function without standards, but the standards would be crafted by individual schools and communities subject only to the requirement that the standards be public and accessible both to members of the school community and to outsiders. Meier believes that such a process would hardly lead to anarchy. Children and parents are already subjected to many outside demands, not the least of which is the need to find jobs in an increasingly credentialized world. But it would free schools up to craft approaches that are more likely to succeed in this world, and the emphasis on democratic practices instills other traits that are needed for schools to enable broader social reform.

Meier describes an experiment in Harlem in which parents were "free to choose a public school that had the curriculum, faculty and spirit that was best for their child. Parents, students and teachers created communities where they could get to know each other well and work closely toward shared goals. Teachers in such schools are required to exercise intelligence rather than expected to dutifully implement other peoples' mandates."[32] Meier's experiment was stunningly successful. More than 90 percent of incoming ninth-graders stayed until graduation, and about 90 percent of the graduates went on to some form of post-secondary education.

Meier certainly does not claim that her curriculum, personnel choices, or graduation requirements would work for all students and parents. But that is exactly her point. She argues that since Dewey's day, and even more so today, we have needed to throw away the "dystopia of the ant colony, the smoothly functioning (and quietly humming) factory where everything goes according to plan, and replace it with the messy, often rambunctious community, with its multiple demands and complicated trade-offs."[33]

Once parents, students, and teachers are empowered to craft standards and design appropriate strategies, different groups may well come up with opposing or partially divergent educational ideals. Nevertheless, the outcome will be healthier in the long run. Parents, students, and teachers will be more committed to achieving those ends because they had a voice in crafting them. In addition, the opportunity to craft individual approaches will stimulate innovation and further reflection. In such a climate, schools will need to remake themselves and still provide sufficient routine and stability. Some may go too far in one direction or another, but they will learn from each other and provide a new balance.

The process of democratic engagement within our schools and the establishment of different schools in the process will teach two fundamental lessons that the commitment to uniform standards enforced by experts subverts. It will deepen a commitment to democracy and foster a higher degree of tolerance for others and even for uncertainty and change.

The practices of such schools do not guarantee effective democratic challenge to the incursions of corporate life, but they do create more fertile soil. To the extent that the reach of corporate life can be curbed, deeper and more widespread opportunities for educational innovation can emerge.

Other educational reformers have supported Meier's conclusions. Larry Cuban, a professor of education at Stanford University, argues that schools can differ dramatically in the ways teachers organize their classrooms, view learning, and teach the curriculum. He cites the example of two vastly different schools—one a traditional school where drills, report cards, and grades are emphasized, and the other a nontraditional school where classrooms are multi-aged, student-initiated projects are emphasized, and no grades are given. Both schools, though different, have achieved enviable records by most measures. What they share are involved parents who believe in and have chosen the schools, have input into their policies, and have recruited teachers who share the commitment to the goals of the school. Cuban concludes that schools excel when they have "stable staffs committed to core beliefs about what is best for students and the community, dedicated parents whose beliefs mirror those of the staff, competent people who work well together, and time to make it happen."[34]

I believe that adequately funded and broadly participatory opportunities for choice within the public-school system over the next few years would lead to some schools that are not only progressive in the ways identified by Cuban but that would also adopt homework policies that reflect some of the principles discussed in this book. Homework would be eliminated in the early grades. For older students, opportunities for independent work in a school or school-like setting would be offered at least as an optional alternative to traditional homework at home. And for all students and teachers the need for some free time would increasingly be recognized.

Parents have asked me on many occasions how to advance an agenda that limits homework. Perhaps the first place to start is by recognizing that the problems many parents and children experience with homework are not individual failings. It is clear that for many years parents have suffered in silence, simply assuming that they were not smart enough or sufficiently well organized to handle the assignments. Those who experience difficulties need to begin by talking with other parents about the burdens homework imposes. Fortunately, such conversations have already begun in many communities.

Once common problems are spotted, parents often go to individual teachers to seek changes. Nevertheless, even when groups of parents are expressing concerns, the visit to individual teachers can be unsatisfying. Administrators and school boards generally impose expectations for or limits on homework.

Parents are most likely to succeed when they can go as a group to school boards and address homework as a legitimate political issue that involves not only pedagogy but also the broad interests of children and parents. Academic expertise is important, but such expertise is not the only guide in this discussion. In any case, as we have seen, the academic case for homework is at best contestable. Parents should be prepared both to call to boards' attention the weakness of this case and to suggest alternative strategies for educational gains. The very process of mobilizing around an issue of widespread concern can build confidence and help in the further efforts to implement alternatives.

Teachers are also an important part of this equation. One author cannot and should not try to specify how teachers should manage their classroom time or provide and monitor the independent work that will replace homework. That is and will be the task of professional educators. Like the rest of us, teachers are creatures of habit. From their own days in elementary school and later, most teachers were assigned homework as students. In their professional training as teachers, assigning homework was the norm, and that norm has often been reinforced by years of assigning homework themselves. For many teachers, asking for major reforms or limitations on homework will almost certainly involve the requirement that they conduct their own working lives in very different ways.

However justified such requests may be in terms of homework's less than stellar track record or its deleterious effects on children or family lives, there is no getting around the fact that teachers will have to make major changes. New resources and opportunities for teacher training and development will have to be part of this package. Nevertheless, bringing teachers and the educational establishment on board will involve showing teachers that homework-free classrooms are already the norm for a minority within the teaching profession, that such classrooms are successful, and that such an approach either has been or could be practiced across different age groups and subject areas.

For starters, we need to put aside some familiar objections to homework-free schools. Some parents I have spoken with worry that eliminating homework removes the parent from ongoing contact with the school. In fact, such elimination could enhance parent–school contact. Parents freed from assisting in lessons with which they may or may not be able help can 1) attend periodic meetings either as individuals or groups with teachers, who are themselves relieved of some of paper-grading burdens; and 2) come to classroom settings under certain circumstances, see the class in action, and so on.

Parents can contribute in other, more substantial ways to their children's education. Robert Moses points out that taking a middle-school child on a trip indirectly introduces concepts of distance, direction, and speed.[35] Taking children to work can also provide them with important information about the organization of work, the design of public space, and the modes of transit available. All such parent-provided experience can be an important subject for classroom discussion.

Does the requirement that high-school students do independent work trap the capable student or the one with parents who can truly help in school when he or she might like to be able to go home and work and could do so with no loss or even academic gain? Under such circumstances, teachers can establish that a student is capable of gaining in this situation and it should be allowed. The point of reforming homework is to provide more opportunity, and certainly such questions are legitimate and changes can be made and negotiated.

Educators are hardly a monolith in support of homework as an educational-enhancement strategy. The pressures on the schools have led some teachers to assign more homework to meet increasing community demands, but many other teachers recognize that homework could still leave them responsible if goals are not achieved in the long run. Or homework controversies could lead to a blame game that benefits no one.

Teachers working on homework-free classroom models have organized their lessons quite differently.[36] In a conventional lesson, a math teacher reviewed homework, demonstrated how to solve the problem of the day, gave students classroom practice, corrected that work, and assigned homework. An alternative approach is to review the previous material, present the problem of the day, and set the students to working on its solution either individually or in groups. The class then discusses solutions (some problems have more than one), often led from the blackboard by students who think they have successfully solved the problem. Outside the class structure, students can work in groups in math labs, generally with access to either older peer tutors or trained adults.

Foreign languages, often cited as an area in which the practice provided by homework is indispensable, are regarded by many teachers today as especially suitable to a de-emphasis on or redefinition of homework. Practicing vocabulary and pronunciation at home in fact can entrench mistakes and kill interests. School-centered language labs provide useful tapes and access to other students with whom practice sessions can be more rewarding and enjoyable. Once again, peer tutors can play a vital role.

Social-studies teachers have used class time not only to present general information to the entire class but also to break classes up into small groups, with each group assigned either a short op-ed piece on a controversial topic or a primary-source document. Each group is responsible for working on a summary or critique of the document at hand, with time later spent reporting to the group as a whole. Once again, assistance is available to the group through teachers and through other trained personnel outside class.

Advocates of broader choice within the public schools would be the last to argue that opening homework-free schools and classrooms, even with appropriately trained teachers and small classes—as important as they are—amount to an educational panacea. Meier and many other educational reformers recognize that the effects of socioeconomic inequality go well beyond school-funding formulas. Children enjoy vastly disparate opportunities for after-school activities as well as vacations. Most of a child's waking hours are spent outside of school settings. Affluent parents spend thousands of dollars to provide opportunities for their children in music, art, and athletics. After-school programs in many communities are beginning to provide analogous opportunities for poor and working-class children, but well-funded programs are the exception.

School-reform packages that emphasize more equal and adequate resources for local schools and more student, parent, and teacher input can provide an occasion for the broader forms of political mobilization. Educational reform that both improves the quality of public schools and fosters the opportunity for more free time for some families at least opens up further political possibilities. It conveys the message that appropriately crafted public policy and a democratically managed and chastened public sector can enhance rather than limit opportunities for personal freedom as both more leisure and more opportunities for recreation, religion, and culture. Cuban recently pointed out that "more Head Start programs, better housing, added health services and increased job training are just a few initiatives found in scores of federal and state programs that can be consolidated and coordinated through schools to help families."[37]

These initiatives in turn might foster and be aided by related community-based pushes on corporate working hours and minimum-wage campaigns. These would dramatically improve the economic circumstances of the adults who make such a difference in the other four-fifths of children's lives. The research on very-early-childhood development confirms views parents have had for generations. The *New York Times* reports: "It turns out, too, that the everyday things parents do with young children, the baby-talk and the peek-a-boo, the kisses and the jokes, are far more subtle and intricate than was previously thought. They appear intricately designed to teach babies just the things they need, in a way that electronic toys or videos can't begin to approach."[38] The *Times* goes on to suggest both that caring for children is important in and of itself and that this insight has profound policy implications:

> Babies and children need time and attention from people who care about them. But society has changed so much in the past 30 years that it is hard for even middle-class parents to meet

these needs, much less the parents of the 20 percent of children raised in poverty. As a society, America simply does not provide support for rearing children. This may well have adverse consequences for children when they grow up—and it undeniably hurts them now.[39]

The *Times* then comments favorably on initiatives that would make it easier for parents to spend time with their young children. It concludes with the warning that

> ultimately, neither children nor childhood itself will be treated with the respect and care they deserve unless the way they are valued changes. Children are the one thing most parents can (and do) give their lives for. One of the few nearly universal moral convictions is that children, in general, deserve protection and care and a chance to learn. Yet that value only seems to count in the public realm if it is expressed as a means to higher test scores or a more competitive labor force or less crowded prisons.[40]

The irony, of course, is that even long-term educational goals are poorly served when children and parents are treated as automata who can and should be ceaselessly worked. Progressive teacher organizations and school reformers who can lend support to family leave and minimum-wage and hours reforms stand to gain not only more respect from many working families but a social environment that is more conducive to their own success.

In this context, my work on homework leads me to believe that the dilemmas parents face are compounded by another component of the standards craze: the demand that students do more homework. Modern school's emphasis on homework places those students without access to libraries, computers, and formally educated parents at a considerable disadvantage. Independent schoolwork is important for the development of young students, especially from high school on. Nevertheless, if such work is not to be an occasion for exacerbating inequalities, it ought to be done within the framework and facilities of the public school. Part of equal funding for education should be the funding of after-school tutors, including not only formally trained teachers but also other skilled community members who can assist students in the learning process.

More broadly, I believe that parents have been increasingly denied input into their children's development in ways that go beyond questions of access to school bureaucracies. Very long hours worked by parents, coupled with the increasing burden of homework on both the parent and the child, means that parents have little time or energy left to engage their children in ways that are not dominated by the school. Much of the enrichment alluded to above once was—and could be again—provided by parents. The unstructured activities of family life—whether in the form of games or learning of specific skills such as cooking and sewing—enhance children's creativity. Parents at all levels of formal education can make distinctive contributions along these lines. But for such developments to occur, reasonable limits need to be placed on the amount of work demanded both by our schools and our workplaces.

Many educational bureaucrats and business leaders jump to the conclusion that opposition to standardized tests, demands to limit working and homework hours, and calls for more corporate democratization amount to a willingness to let everything go. Such arguments were launched against unions and the forty-hour workweek in the 1930s.

The same logic is especially evident today in a range of educational debates. Indeed, education is made the whipping boy for the insecurities and inequities that characterize even our current prosperity. If there is not one uniform, clear, and easily quantifiable academic measure–administered by experts–schools will be chaotic, and laziness will reign supreme.

But schools such as Meier's do not lack standards. At their best, these schools evaluate students and teachers using a number of criteria. Standardized tests may play some role, but they are hardly the lodestone by which all success is measured. Standards themselves are periodically evaluated and flexibly applied. Rather than an excuse for laziness, flexible standards and some unstructured time offer a continuous challenge to teachers, parents, and students. There is much to suggest that this approach brings out the best in students and future citizens.

Accountability within a more equally and adequately funded public-school system can be achieved by giving parents more choices within that system. With more adequate funding for smaller classes and better teacher training, public-school systems would offer more options. Charter schools working within the public-school system might experiment with collaboratively designed evaluation systems for teachers, staff, and students. Fashioning more equal and more open public schools will be the best way both to advance education and to restore faith in democracy.

Conclusion

On Character and Public Education in Democratic Society

IN RECENT books, articles, and public appearances, I have argued that the policies our public schools adopt toward homework need to be rethought. Homework does not convey the academic benefits its proponents promise. It also creates inordinate difficulties for children from poor economic backgrounds. Just as fundamentally, all children, just like adults, deserve some time and space of their own. Elementary-school children already work nearly thirty hours a week in school, and they often spend another five hours a week commuting to their workplaces. The studies showing that homework benefits these children are tenuous at best and are countered by other studies indicating that homework at this age can even be counterproductive. Independent work for older students is very important, but it should be carried on in a school setting, where all students can have access to trained adults and a safe, secure, and well-equipped environment. Even for these older students, reasonable limits need to be negotiated.

Needless to say, these arguments have evoked intense responses, all the way from "Right on! I have wanted someone to say this for a long time" to the suggestion that my argument amounts to the further "dumbing down" of education just because a few cannot meet the rigors of school.

I often point out that I am not in favor of reducing standards and that the argument is over the means by which standards are to be met. Smaller classes, better teacher training, more access to pre-kindergarten training, and appropriately structured programs for independent projects by older students would achieve far better results than ratcheting up homework.

At this point some of my more liberal critics generally suggest, "Well, we ought to put more money in schools and ask more of our children and our schools." They argue that whatever the dueling studies may suggest, the risk-free and common-sense course is to require homework. It may work, after all, and even if it is not working now, surely we can design homework regimes that will.

Once the argument moves beyond dueling studies regarding the efficacy of homework, the debate then makes a subtle shift. Even if homework is not as academically valuable as we once thought, it teaches important life skills. Homework builds character. The argument that homework's academic defenders make on this score resonates among some of the broader public. As Mike Rosen, the host of a talk show on the radio station KOA in Denver, put it to me during an interview, homework teaches children that "life involves doing things you don't want to do."

For the most ardent advocates of homework, the social costs of homework criticism are immense and are all around us. One reviewer for the magazine *National Review* charged:

"Homework is not a threat to our civilization–but the anti-homework movement surely is."[1] In more flamboyant language, John Silber commented: "Kralovec and Buell also argue without embarrassment that the principal task facing adolescents is not learning but becoming socially adept. An illiterate high school graduate skilled at making pickups in bars would, on their terms, be an educational success."[2]

Thus, the debate for many is not merely–or even primarily–over the role that homework plays in acquiring a set of cognitive skills. It is an argument about character broadly conceived.

My opposition to homework intensification springs not merely from a different reading of the academic literature on homework but also from this larger issue of character and how it is formed. In the first place, I believe that the primary job of the schools is to teach literacy and numeracy. These goals put some limits on the range of acceptable character, but they still leave considerable latitude. Students must not disrupt others or engage in violent acts, and even in my program students are not endlessly coddled. They must remain on task during the school day. Teachers pose more difficult and challenging tasks for students as they age, albeit in a context where advice and support are available.

I believe that the socially necessary forms of self-discipline are more likely to emerge in a setting where challenges are not overwhelming and where students who work hard can know they have a reasonable chance of periodic success. Failure is part of learning and life, but continual failure in the face of overwhelming odds breeds cynicism and despair, not self-direction. When Isaac Newton remarked of his work, "I stand upon the shoulders of giants," he had a surer grasp of the origins of genius than many of the contemporary advocates of tough love.

Yet character and self-discipline do involve more than the ability to achieve basic skills or even solve difficult intellectual problems. My conception of the sort of self-discipline appropriate to a modern democratic society is very different from Bempechat's, Silber's, and Rosen's.

I should preface my remarks by saying first that for advocates of hard empirical reasoning of the sort these authors profess to be, their comments on suffering are curiously rhetorical. How much do modern children suffer, and even if homework were removed, what levels of suffering would remain? I am far from confident that I can place a precise register on suffering. For human beings, it clearly includes more than merely a physical component. Even in physical terms, however, substantial numbers of our children suffer by almost any standard. About 20 percent of American children live below the federal government's official poverty line, a level set so low that it excludes even the most minimal middle-class necessities. For many children, living below the poverty line translates into frequently coming to school inadequately fed and being unable to find even a quiet and secure space in which to do academic work at home, even if the time is available.

Working-class children do not suffer abject poverty, but most today grow up concerned that they will not be able to occupy even the same kind of jobs and benefits on which their parents have a tenuous hold. Most are already working as teenagers and face longer odds in terms of affording college than did their peers two decades ago. A 1998 study by the National Research Council and the Institute of Medicine found that teenagers working more than twenty hours per week had lower grades, greater alcohol use, and less time with their parents and families. The work also affects their futures. The study found that "young people who worked long hours during high school are more likely to have lower educational attainment a decade later than those who did not."[3] It is commonplace to point out that only a minority of the children working after school do so in order to meet financial needs of the family, but even this calculation fails to consider the financial pressures on children considering college. In addition, even when work is directed toward a car or better clothes, such desires themselves can reflect, as Schor has indicated, the continuing pressures for consumption and display built into adult culture, the media, and even the school environment.

Nor is there much evidence that modern parents are "coddling" their children. For much of the past decade, many have been leading the charge both for tougher school standards and more homework—all to prepare children for a future many working-class parents may deplore on some level but now often regard as inevitable.

Even for middle-class children, Bempechat's picture of coddled youth grows out of stereotypes based on 1960s extremes rather than the practices and expectations of today. Many of today's middle-class parents are attempting to turn their children into great minds right from the crib. A growing market in "smart toys" is designed to improve the mental capacity of children well before they enter even preschool programs. Several commentators have suggested—some with amusement and others with alarm—that many parents are convinced they can turn children into smart adults by giving them toys with scientific-sounding names right from the cradle.

These goals and pressures continue into all stages of childhood. The demands on parents plus the requirements they feel compelled to impose on their children have had major implications for the structure of children's lives. A careful study of how time is used by children sees major changes in the last two decades. These researchers conclude: "We see the composition of children's free time changing. Less time is now spent in unstructured activities such as playing and passive activities such as television viewing and more time is spent in structured activities such as art and sports and in educational activities such as studying and reading."[4] What this means in concrete terms has been vividly conveyed by admissions officers at Harvard, where Bempechat once taught:

> The competition for admission to some of the Pre-K, Kindergarten, and grammar schools can be intense–statistically more difficult (with lower admission rates) than Harvard. Once in the "right" school, students are pushed along by teachers, by outside tutors and, if they stumble, by learning specialists who will help them approach their studies in the most efficient manner. The school day continues well into the night with structured study time and drills. The pressure can be relentless, even from well-intentioned parents.[5]

Harvard administrators then go on to describe the consequences of this agenda, especially as it becomes a life long imperative:

> Faced with the fast pace of growing up today, some students are clearly distressed, engaging in binge drinking and other self-destructive behaviors. Counseling services of secondary schools and colleges have expanded in response to greatly increased demand. It is common to encounter even the most successful students, who have won all the "prizes," stepping back and wondering if it was all worth it. Professionals in their thirties and forties–physicians, lawyers, academics, business people and others–sometimes give the impression

that they are dazed survivors of some bewildering life-long boot-camp. Some say they ended up in their profession because of someone else's expectations, or that they simply drifted into it without pausing to think whether they really loved their work. Often they say they missed their youth entirely, never living in the present, always pursuing some ill-defined future goal.[6]

Just as I suspect advocates of tough homework and standards have inadequately addressed existing stress, I also cannot recognize my position in the educational conservatives' characterization of me. The 1960s surely had some—though even this is exaggerated—for whom a do-your-own-thing morality was regarded as appropriate for schools and workplaces. But may one legitimately infer from such historical experience that anyone who argues that schoolwork needs to be limited so that children may engage in other activities thereby advocates that all the challenge and hardship be taken out of schools or more broadly social life? Such a reading assumes that only academic work entails hardship and defeat.

I suspect that if most parents reflect on their experiences in sharing a hobby with a child or in supervising household chores, they would be hard pressed to argue that there was not much frustration and disappointment through which the child had to work. I believe that self-discipline, however conceived, has more plural origins than homework's ardent defenders acknowledge.

Yet on the most fundamental level, I deny the stark dichotomy with which my critics confront me. One is not left to choose between a world of self-indulgence on the one hand, where the child is relieved of every possible burden and disappointment the parent can manage, and a world where the child is expected perpetually to measure up to extraordinarily difficult cognitive and moral challenges. Self-discipline does not mean primarily learning that life is tough and that one must generally do what one is told. It means learning to manage freedom.

Freedom's precondition does lie in the challenging work that provides the affluence on which any leisure activity must rest. But a life led in continual deference to work is neither self-disciplined nor free. Perhaps none of us was designed neatly to fit any one pattern, however compelling and clear that pattern may seem now. As even some of the most sophisticated theories in physics and ecology now suggest, the world may be too complex, unpredictable, and protean to be defined by one singular purpose, even work. Freedom is possible only through a continual process of negotiation both within others and ourselves. A life led in obeisance to chores leaves no space for the unpredictable moments of aesthetic and personal pleasure in life, but a life led in continual quest of personal pleasures however defined can destroy not only others but ourselves. There is no precise midpoint that can be defined as to the perfect and permanent balance of personal freedom and social obligation. Part of social and personal maturity is learning to accept–and even relish–the need and opportunity to make periodic readjustments both as our life circumstances change and as social conditions, technology, and science itself evolve around us. Maturity involves not only acceptance of but also glorying in the need to make periodic social and personal adjustments along this fundamental register of our being.

I resent homework intensification not because I am lazy or want to spare children all challenges and difficulties but because I want to instill the character and self-discipline I admire. I want children to have gradually expanding opportunities both to manage and be responsible for free time.

We have all heard that children already have too much free time and that they spend endless hours in front of televisions and computers. I believe that children's time is shrinking and not expanding when one considers homework, time spent commuting to schools, the number of extracurricular activities middle-class children are bound to add to their high-school résumés, paid jobs that increasing numbers of even middle-class children do, and household chores. And many parents fear children's freedom and seek to monitor and micromanage much of even older teens lives.

There is too much TV time, but much of this is passive and escapist in large measure because children are tired and have too few opportunities for self-chosen recreational and cultural activities. The very effort to teach self-discipline by continually imposing tasks often backfires in mindless resistance to all authority. Silber has done little to assess the social origins of the bar-hopping and sexual adventurism he deplores.

In a recent commentary on youth delinquency in Great Britain, the *Guardian* assessed the rise of urban graffiti in ways that have clear implications for U.S. problems and concerns. "Graffiti and vandalism are . . . linked with a lack of things to do and places to go for young people without money in both urban and rural areas. Local authorities have seen endless budget cuts over recent decades and youth activities, leisure services, libraries, clubs, have all suffered severely. Schools and councils have been forced to sell off playing fields and open spaces where kids might have let off steam."[7]

It is at least worth considering that such types of destructive or dangerous behavior emerge from an educational system and culture that denies adequate opportunities to its poorest and imposes relentless pressures and expectations on even its best and brightest. Workaholism and its frequent twin, an obsessive opposition to all forms of pleasure may in fact have bred their mindless mirror image in Silber's bar stalker.

In this regard, it is worth re-examining the lessons that might be learned from drug and alcohol policy. A mindless, just-say-no war on alcohol among teenagers has helped inspire a binge-drinking clientele on many college campuses. It might also be worth noting that both France and Italy, where attitudes toward both work and alcohol are more relaxed than in the United States, have far fewer problems with alcohol abuse than do our college campuses.

Consider for a moment the voice of fifteen-year-old Mark: "We've got superparents who raised superkids and were working so hard, and we hate all this pressure. I mean, my sister, who's in second grade, is at one of these hot girls' schools and has two hours of homework a night. She cries about it, and I have to help her, 'cause my parents are out a lot. And what is it all for? To go to Harvard or Yale or maybe Bowdoin if you aren't so lucky, to work your butt off at some law firm just to become another superparent raising superkids."[8]

This teenager may choose to opt out of the professional corporate culture. But will he become Silber's bar stalker? No one can say for sure, but his options will depend heavily not merely on his inner character and choices but also on the economic opportunities available and even the reigning moral dialogue of the culture. Unless he is fortunate enough to inherit substantial wealth from his superparents, he faces difficult choices. Today, those who do not make it in the jet-set corporate world face an ever more uncertain future. Yes, some can and do carve out survival strategies, but the shrinking safety net, the ever lower pay of most part-time jobs, the more repressive state apparatus that frowns on underground activities and the unauthorized use of vacant buildings and open forestland all make such strategies more tenuous. Deprived of any mode of secure subsistence, he may turn to various forms of dangerous escapism. Even he may someday regret that he did not push himself hard enough at least to get into Bowdoin.

But even if he were to toe the line and succeed, success in today's terms might take its toll. Just as plausible as Silber's scenario is a picture of the bar stalker as burned-out corporate man, one who mortgaged all of his childhood and early-adult years to the dream and could not sustain the costs it exacted.

One may read a more hopeful voice in this fifteen-year-old—a voice that, while not denying central moral purposes and goals, asks that they be kept in perspective and open to negotiation in the interest of a greater recognition of human complexity, of what Walt Whitman called the multitudes we all may contain.

Because I believe in character formation and yet hold views different from Silber's as to what good character is and how to achieve it, I want a measure of this in my hands. Schools and parents who seek long homework hours not primarily because of the skills it imparts but because of the character it instills are impinging on my parental rights.

By the same token, I would not seek to impose on theirs. The beauty of the homework reforms I advocate is that they do not impose one model of character. Some parents define character in more religious terms and would like religious education to be a broader part of their children's lives. Although I am bothered by many fundamentalist versions of religion and by those that advocate strict and very narrow standards of sexual probity, I also endorse the right of parents to convey that message. The beauty of homework reform is that it frees more time for parents to concentrate on the kind of character education they most value. Even those parents who define character primarily in terms of a continuing commitment to academic learning are and should be free to impose academic tasks of their own, to go to teachers to seek more work that they can oversee and direct with their children.

Though I fear for these children, just as their parents fear for mine, I believe both sets of parents are more likely in the long run to live in peace with each other and with the public schools if each can have a broader say in character education for their children. Such freedoms for both sets of parents are strengthened even more within the context of reforms that would allow parents to design and model schools that imposed or did not impose strict homework requirements.

How would the public or independent schools that I might counsel advance true democratic education? I believe democratic education needs to be liberal in its willingness to expose students to a range of ideologies, moral systems, and culture, and it needs to be broadly participatory. Although these goals are both vital, one would be naive to assume that there are never any tensions between them. Parents need to be involved in charting the education of their children, but for too many parents today education can often amount to ideological and moral indoctrination. Nor can education mean special favors to some children at the expense of the many—education that in essence serves the loudest mouths.

Nevertheless, the answer to these disturbing trends does not lie in attempting to shut parents out of educational-policy formation. Such exclusion is likely only to intensify the resentment and anger that foster various forms of educational fundamentalism. Rather, one should strive to make the process fully democratic. Teachers and administrators should acknowledge the absolute importance of parental participation but insist that such participation be truly democratic. A voice in broader public discussion of school policy and aims is appropriate, but such sessions should strive for openness of discourse and broad discussion of the implications of individual demands for the whole school population. Teachers need to be part of the mix, for a school that overworks and abuses its teachers is unlikely to sustain the kind of civil disagreements that are a crucial part of learning.

What about the broader curriculum of such schools? I have already discussed the need for and possibility of homework-free classrooms, but the direction of education itself must prepare future citizens of our democracy. Math and science instruction, often the focus of those who see education as primarily a source of good jobs, deserves to be emphasized. Nevertheless, its focus must be more than good jobs. When such education is well done, it can make students aware of the role that math and science play in a whole range of current public-policy controversies that will affect the quality of their lives. These include such persistent issues as the greenhouse effect, the Human Genome Project, the war on cancer, and alternative energy.

Education in the social sciences must strive to make students aware of the range of ideological debates regarding such notions as economic freedom, political equality, and the role that disputed understandings of race and gender play. The formation process and the travails of dissident understandings of individual and group identities must be an important theme in literature classes and within history and social-science discourse.

Ideally, such a curriculum should provide students and faculty with ample opportunities for interdisciplinary courses and projects, an aim that may be facilitated through adequate opportunities for professional development of staff and provision of time within the school day for faculty to work and plan together. In addition, the multicultural emphasis in the curriculum can be both supplemented and enriched to the extent that students and parents take advantage of the greater free time offered for a range of informal exchanges with other schools and communities.

For changes of this sort to happen, the politics of time within our workplaces and schools must be a crucial topic of debate within both our schools and the larger political culture. Democratic education seeks to expose students to a variety of views, but parents who are overworked themselves tend the most to cling defensively to their own values and identities and to be most resistant to exploring alternative mindsets. By the same token, giving parents some space of their own, and the chance to engage in a variety of cultural, recreational, and family-related activities of their own choosing, can relax such pressures.

Students can and will study hard if they are given well-trained teachers who can make efficient use of the existing school day. Older students can also benefit from independent work in a safe, secure, and well-equipped school setting where they have access to trained staff. But both students and parents are most likely to engage in fulfilling work, become democratic citizens, and enjoy a high quality of life when each also knows that schools and workplaces do not entail work without end.

My hope is that education might nurture democratic citizenship. The democratic citizen must cooperate with others in crafting the common standards and social supports on which all civilized life depends. But democracy also entails a commitment to individuality, to resistance even to widely shared norms whose cost in the loss of free space is greater than any social benefits. It entails a willingness to constantly tweak and explore this balance.

Thoreau was such a citizen, and his experience is instructive. We owe Thoreau's great classics not only to the hours he devoted to acquiring a classical education but also to his willingness to spend—indeed, to demand—time and space for totally unstructured wanderings through and contemplation of the minutiae of nature. It may not be accidental that a citizen who had experienced the constantly renegotiated moments of freedom in his own life was willing to engage in civil disobedience, the ultimate in democratic political practice, to secure these values for others.

Notes

Introduction

1. Kate Zernike, "Homework: What's Enough? One District Takes Its Stand," *New York Times,* October 10, 2000, 1, 29.

2. Etta Kralovec and John Buell, *The End of Homework: How Homework Disrupts Families, Overburdens Children, and Limits Learning* (Boston: Beacon Press, 2000).

3. Chloe Bordewich (Red Hook, N.Y.), "Write 100 Times: Give Homework" [letter to the editor], *New York Times,* October 12, 2000, A28; available from: <http://query.nytimes.com/gst/abstract.html?res=F4081EF83C5B0C718DDDA90994D8404482>.

4. Canadian Broadcasting Corporation, *Sunday Edition* [radio program], January 21, 2001.

Chapter One

1. Harris Cooper, *Homework* (White Plains, N.Y.: Longman, 1989), 109.

2. Ibid., 44.

3. For a detailed discussion of these tests, see Peter Sacks, "Testing Times in Higher Education," *The Nation,* June 24, 2002, 25–31.

4. Gerald W. Bracey, "Are U.S. Students Behind?" *American Prospect* [Internet ed.], vol. 9, no. 37, March 1, 1998; available from: <http://www.prospect.org/print/V9/37/bracey-g.html>.

5. As reported in Lonnie Golden and Helene Jorgensen, "Time after Time: Mandatory Overtime in the U.S. Economy," Economic

Policy Institute Briefing Paper, Executive Summary, January 2002; available from: <http://www.epinet.org/briefingpapers/120/bp120.pdf>.

6. Harris Cooper, "Synthesis of Research on Homework," *Educational Leadership*, vol. 47, no. 3 (1989): 89.

7. Cooper, *Homework*, 189; emphasis added.

8. Michelle Ingrassia, "Homework Backlash," *New York Daily News*, October 22, 2000, 2–3.

9. Susan Ohanian, *One Size Fits Few* (Portsmouth, N.H.: Heinemann, 1999), 18.

10. Noah Adams and Linda Wertheimer [hosts] and Michelle Trudeau [reporter], "Profile: Psychological, Intellectual and Emotional Differences between Teens and Adults as It Pertains to How to Punish Teen-agers for Crimes They Commit," report on National Public Radio, *All Things Considered*, February 13, 2001.

11. Barbara Kantrowitz and Pat Wingert, "Doctor's Orders," *Newsweek*, October 2, 2000, 43–47.

12. For discussion of these themes, see Mel Levine, *One Mind at a Time* (New York: Simon and Schuster, 2002), esp. chaps. 1 and 2.

13. Kathy Seal, "Too Much Homework, Too Little Play," *New York Times*, September 3, 2001, A15; available from: <http://query.nytimes.com/gst/abstract.html?res=F00817FD3A540C708CDDA00894D9404482>. Deborah Stipek and Kathy Seal, *Motivated Minds: Raising Children to Love Learning* (New York: Owl Books, 2001).

14. This experiment is cited in William Connolly, *Neuropolitics: Thinking, Culture, Speed* (Minneapolis: University of Minnesota Press, 2002), 32.

15. Ibid., 91; emphasis added.

16. As quoted in Gerald Bracey, "What They Did on Vacation," *Washington Post*, January 16, 2002, A19.

17. Connolly, *Neuropolitics*, 143.

18. Arthur Levine, "Tomorrow's Education Made to Measure," *New York Times*, December 22, 2000, A33.

Chapter Two

1. Barbara Kantrowitz and Pat Wingert, "The Parent Trap," *Newsweek*, January 29, 2001, 49–53.

2. James Lardner, "World-Class Workaholics," *U.S. News and World Report*, December 20, 1999, 44–45.

3. Ibid., 42.

4. E. P. Thompson, "Time, Work Discipline, and Industrial Capitalism," *Past and Present* 38 (December 1967): 56–97.

5. Benjamin Kline Hunnicutt, *Work without End* (Philadelphia: Temple University Press, 1988), 12.

6. Herbert Gutman, *Work, Culture, and Society in Industrializing America* (New York: Alfred A. Knopf, 1976), 38 ff.

7. Thompson, "Time," 84.

8. Juliet Schor, *The Overworked American* (New York: Basic Books, 1991), 74.

9. Samuel Bowles and Herbert Gintis, *Schooling in Capitalist America: Educational Reform and the Contradictions of Economic Life* (New York: Basic Books, 1976), 167–69.

10. Brian Gill and Steve Schlossman, "A Sin against Childhood: Progressive Education and the Crusade to Abolish Homework, 1897–1941," *American Journal of Education,* vol. 105, no. 1 (November 1996): 30.

11. William H. Burnham, "The Hygiene of Home Study," *Pedagogical Seminary* 12 (June 1905): 213. This article was originally published in *Discussions in Education* (New York, 1899), 239–40.

12. Vivian T. Thayer. *The Passing of Recitation* (Boston: D. C. Heath, 1928).

13. Edward Bok, "A National Crime at the Feet of American Parents," *Ladies Home Journal,* vol. 17, no. 2 (January 1900), 16.

14. Ibid.; idem, "The First Blow," *Ladies Home Journal,* vol. 17, no. 11 (October 1900), 16; idem, "First Step to Change the Public Schools," *Ladies Home Journal,* vol. 31, no. 1 (January 1912), 3–4.

15. John Dewey, *The School and Society* (Chicago: University of Chicago Press, 1915); Carleton Washburne, "How Much Homework?" *Parent's Magazine,* vol. 12, no. 11 (November 1937), 16–17, 68–71.

16. William H. Holmes, "Home Work Is School Work Out of Place," *American Childhood* 152 (October 1929): 5–7, 55–56.

17. Hunnicutt, *Work without End,* 118.

18. Ibid.

19. Ibid., 120.

20. Clara Bassett, *The School and Mental Health* (New York: Commonwealth Fund, 1934).

21. Dacie Harvey, "Too Much Homework," *New York Times,* April 4, 1935, 22.

22. Jay B. Nash, "At What Price Home Study?" *School Parent,* vol. 93, no. 5 (May 31, 1930): 6, 12.

23. Janine Bempechat, *Getting Our Kids Back on Track: Educating Children for the Future* (San Francisco: Jossey-Bass, 2000).

24. Gerald W. Bracey, "Are U.S. Students Behind?" *American Prospect* [Internet ed.], vol. 9, no. 37, March 1, 1998; available from: <http://www.prospect.org/print/V9/37/bracey-g.html>.

25. For this line of thought, I am indebted to Michael Sherry, *In the Shadow of War* (New Haven, Conn.: Yale University Press, 1995), 214–33, and David Campbell, *Writing Security* (Minneapolis: University of Minnesota Press, 1998).

26. Schor, *Overworked American*, 78.

27. P. R. Wildman, "Homework Pressures," *Peabody Journal of Education*, vol. 45, no. 4 (January 1968): 204.

28. Ibid.

29. U.S. Department of Education, *A Nation at Risk: The Imperative of Educational Reform* (Washington, D.C.: U.S. Department of Education, 1983), 5.

30. Schor, *Overworked American*, 152.

31. See Juliet Schor, *The Overspent American: Upscaling, Downshifting, and the New Consumer* (New York: Basic Books, 1998).

32. Susan Ohanian, *One Size Fits Few* (Portsmouth, N.H.: Heinemann, 1999), 104.

33. Schor, *Overspent American*, 97.

34. Ibid., 120.

35. I tell part of this story in John Buell, *Democracy by Other Means: The Politics of Work, Culture, and Environment* (Champaign: University of Illinois Press, 1995), and in John Buell and Thomas DeLuca, *Sustainable Democracy: Individuality and the Politics of the Environment* (Thousand Oaks, Calif.: Sage, 1997).

Chapter Three

1. Richard DuBoff, "Globalization and Wages: The Downward Escalator," *Dollars and Sense* (September–October 1997), 40.

2. Harley Shaiken, *Work Transformed: Automation and Labor in the Computer Age* (Lexington, Mass.: Lexington Books, 1985).

3. Lester C. Thurow, *The Future of Capitalism: How Today's Economic Forces Shape Tomorrow's World* (New York: William Morrow, 1996).

4. I discuss this example in John Buell, *Democracy by Other Means: The Politics of Work, Culture, and Environment* (Champaign: University of Illinois Press, 1995), chap. 2.

5. Richard DuBoff, "Technology and Skills: Up or Down," *Dollars and Sense* (January–February 2000), 34.

6. Susan Ohanian, *One Size Fits Few* (Portsmouth, N.H.: Heinemann, 1999), 113–14.

7. Merrill Lynch, "General Electric Company," investment advisory, December 14, 1999, 95.

8. Jonathan Kozol, *Savage Inequalities: Children in America's Schools* (New York: Perennial, 1992).

9. Carl E. Van Horn, "No Longer at the Margins: Working Poor Essential to New Jersey and America's Continuing Prosperity," report, Rutgers University Center for Workforce Development, New Brunswick, N.J., 1999; available from: <http://www.heldrich. rutgers.edu/>.

10. See Economic Policy Institute, "The State of Working America," website; available from: <http://www.epinet.org>.

11. Will Hutton, "Log Cabin to the Whitehouse? Not Any More," *The Observer* (London) [Internet ed.], April 28, 2002; available from: <http://www.commondreams.org>.

12. Richard Herrenstein and Charles Murray, *The Bell Curve: Intelligence and Class in America* (New York: Free Press, 1994).

13. Dean Baker, *Economic Reporting Review*, website, May–June 2002; available from: <http://www.cepr.net/Economic_Reporting_Review/index.htm>.

14. Roy Hattersley, "This Strange Silence from the Left," *The Guardian* (London) [Internet ed.], July 15, 2002; <http://www.guardian.co.uk/comment/story/0,3604,755319,00.html>.

15. David Moberg, "Labor Champions Reform as Big Business Squirms," AlterNet, website, October 10, 2002; available from: <http://www.alternet.org/story.html?StoryID=14279>.

16. Robert D. Putnam, *Bowling Alone: The Collapse and Revival of American Community* (Carmichael, Calif.: Touchstone Books, 2001).

17. Theda Skocpol, "Associations without Members," *American Prospect* [Internet ed.], vol. 10, no. 45, July 1, 1999–August 1, 1999, available from: <http://www.prospect.org/print/V10/45/skocpol-t.html>.

Chapter Four

1. Ryan O'Donnell, letter to the editor, *New York Times,* October 12, 2000.

2. As quoted in Gerald W. Bracey, "Are U.S. Students Behind?" *American Prospect* [Internet ed.], vol. 9, no. 37, March 1, 1998; available from: <http://www.prospect.org/print/V9/37/bracey-g.html>.

3. Ibid.

4. Ibid.

5. Ibid.

6. Ibid.

7. Ibid.

8. Ibid.

9. Leon Botstein, "We Waste Our Children's Time," *New York Times,* January 25, 2001, op-ed section.

10. Gerald W. Bracey, "What Teachers Know," *American Prospect* [Internet ed.], vol. 11, no. 7, February 14, 2000; available from: <http://www.prospect.org/print/V11/7/bracey-g.html>.

11. Ibid.

12. Bracey, "Are U.S. Students Behind?"

13. Etta Kralovec, *Schools That Do Too Much* (Boston: Beacon Press, forthcoming), 34.

14. Ibid., 25.

15. Ibid., 30.

16. Ohanian, *Schools,* 13–14.

17. Kralovec, *Schools,* 77–78.

18. Ibid., 78.

19. David Berliner, "Our Schools vs. Theirs," *Washington Post,* Outlook Section, January 28, 2001.

20. Howard W. French, "More Sunshine for Japan's Overworked Students," *New York Times,* February 25, 2001, 6

21. Martin Carnoy, "Do School Vouchers Improve Student Performance?" *American Prospect,* Internet ed., January 1, 2001.

22. David Grissmer, Ann Flanagan, Jennifer Kawata, and Stephanie Williamson, *Improving Student Achievement: What NAEP State Test Scores Tell Us* (Santa Monica, Calif.: Rand Corporation, 2000), 271.

23. Valerie E. Lee and David T. Burkam, "Inequality at the Starting Gate," Economic Policy Institute, September 2002; available from: <http://www.epinet.org/content.cfm/books_starting_gate>.

24. See Nancy Folbre's discussion of this point in "Leave No Child Behind?" *American Prospect* [Internet ed.], vol. 12, no. 1, January 1, 2001–January 15, 2001; available from: <http://www.prospect.org/print/V12/1/folbre-n.html>.

25. Susan Ohanian, "Standardized Schools," *The Nation,* October 18, 1999, 6–7.

26. Alfie Kohn,"No to Standardized Testing," op-ed, *The Globe* (Boston), May 14, 2001; available from: <http://www.boston.com/globe/>.

27. Ohanian, *One Size Fits Few,* 140.

28. Ibid., 112–13.

29. Kralovec, *Schools,* 54.

30. Barry Bluestone and Bennett Harrison, *Growing Prosperity: The Battle For Growth with Equity in the Twenty-first Century* (Boston: Houghton Mifflin, 2000), 168.

31. Deborah Meier, "Educating a Democracy," *Boston Review,* December 1999, 4–9.

32. Deborah Meier, "Do We Need Educational Standards?" *Boston Review,* December 1999/January 2000, vol. 24, no. 6, 7.

33. Meier, "Educating," 9.

34. Larry Cuban, "Why Bad Reforms Won't Give Us Good Schools," *American Prospect,* January 1, 2001, 48.

35. See the discussion of pedagogy in Robert Moses and Charles E. Cobb, Jr., *Radical Equations: Math Literacy and Civil Rights* (Boston: Beacon Press, 2001), chap. 5.

36. Bracey, "What Teachers Know."

37. Larry Cuban, "Two Decades of School Reform Take Us Back to the 1950s," *Los Angeles Times* [Internet ed.], February 18, 2001; available from: <http://www.latimes.com/>.

38. Alison Gopnik, "Children Need Childhood, Not Vocational Training," *New York Times,* Ideas and Trends section, December 24, 2000, 6.

39. Ibid.

40. Ibid.

Conclusion

1. John T. Gartner, "Training for Life," *National Review,* January 22, 2001, 44.

2. John Silber, "Homework Serves a Purpose," *Boston Herald,* November 2000, 29.

3. Steven Greenhouse, "Problems Seen for Teenagers Who Hold Jobs," *New York Times,* January 29, 200, A1.

4. Sandra Hofferth and John Sandberg, "Changes in Children's Time, 1981–1997," *Children at the Millennium: Where Have We Come from, Where Are We Going?* ed. T. Owens and S. Hofferth, Advances in Life Course Research (New York: Elsevier Science, 2001).

5. William Fitzsimmons, Marlyn McGrath Lewis, and Charles Ducey, "Time Out or Burn Out for the Next Generation," Undergraduate Admissions Office, Harvard University; available from: <http://www.college.harvard.edu/admissions/time_out.html>.

6. Ibid.

7. Judith Williamson, "Tough on Horridness," *The Guardian* [Internet ed.], November 14, 2002; available from: <http://www. guardian.co.uk/comment/story/0,3604,839476,00.html>.

8. This note was forwarded to me by Beacon Press after publication of our first book on homework: Etta Kralovec and John Buell, *The End of Homework: How Homework Disrupts Families, Overburdens Children, and Limits Learning* (Boston: Beacon Press, 2000).

Index